THE TRUE SCHOOL IS LIFE

*Teaching hours with Gabriele,
the prophetess and emissary of God
in our time*

Volume 1

*The eternal Word,
the One God, the Free Spirit,
speaks through Gabriele,
as through all the prophets of God—
Abraham, Job, Moses, Elijah, Isaiah,*

*Jesus of Nazareth,
the Christ of God*

The True School Is Life

*Teaching hours with Gabriele,
the prophetess and emissary of God
in our time*

Volume 1

*"The True School Is Life
Teaching hours with Gabriele,
the prophetess and emissary of God"*

1st Edition, November 2023
© Gabriele-Verlag Das Wort GmbH
Max-Braun-Str. 2, 97828 Marktheidenfeld
www.gabriele-verlag.com
www.gabriele-publishing-house.com

Translated from the original German title:
„Die Wahre Schule ist das Leben – Band 01"

The German edition is the work of reference
for all questions regarding the meaning of the contents.

All rights reserved

Order No. S552TBEN

All decorative letters: © Gabriele-Verlag Das Wort

Printed by: KlarDruck GmbH, Marktheidenfeld, Germany

ISBN 978-3-96446-424-8

Table of Contents

Foreword 7

God Can Be Found 13

What Is True Happiness? 23

The Speaking God 35

Keep the Inner Calm in Every Situation 43

We Greet Spring. We bear within everything that lives. Everything that lives radiates to us and speaks to us 51

Take the Freedom. Become Free—Be Free! 64

Prologues and Monologues 85

The Law of Correspondence 90

The Disease-causing Subconscious and Life 99

The New Person—How Do I Stay True to My Resolutions? 122

*The Language of the Soul via Feelings
and Moods* *130*

*The Christ Telephone—a Hotline for "Please"
and "Thank You"*.. *146*

*Learn to Live with Nature and the Animals,
then You Will Learn to Understand Yourself
and Your Neighbor Better* *154*

Learn to Love, Gain Freedom and Be Happy *176*

Reincarnation and Rebirth in the Spirit.............. *193*

Redemption in Us *201*

Foreword

May the one who can grasp it, grasp it: God, the Eternal, speaks to us today through His prophetess and emissary, Gabriele—and that, for nearly 50 years. He gives revelations as He has at all times: His eternal word of love for God and neighbor through His prophets—from Abraham to Gabriele.

From the Kingdom of God, God-Father, the All-Creator, spoke and speaks through them; the Christ of God, the Co-Regent of the Kingdom of God, spoke and speaks through them; and the Cherub of Divine Wisdom spoke and speaks through them.

The Free Spirit gives revelations on all subjects of life: He gives us insight into our eternal homeland, the Kingdom of God, and into the makeup of our soul; He explains the meaning and purpose of our life on Earth. He teaches the truth about life and the original teachings of Jesus of Nazareth, and gives us people the Inner Path, the path to the liberation of our soul from all that separates us from God.

Hearing or reading a revelation from the Kingdom of God through the teaching prophetess of God, Gabriele, is a key experience for many people—and for the soul, it is often the beginning of the way home, to the eternal homeland from which we once went forth.

What perhaps not many people have experienced is the emissary of God, Gabriele, as a sister who exemplifies the divine laws and gives us an understanding of them with the words from her opened consciousness—the love for God and neighbor toward people, nature and animals that is lived.

In hundreds of teaching hours, seminars and public events, Gabriele has given schoolings on all subjects and spheres of life. She brings the teachings of the Christ of God to us with practical advice on how to implement them in our daily lives, step by step. In these seminars and schoolings, the participants could bring their questions and experiences and, from this, conversations developed with Gabriele, in which she gave help upon help in a wide spectrum, not only for the participants, but for all people, always true to life and in a depth that touches the soul in its innermost being.

Gabriele's words are a road map to the true life, given from the divine Wisdom and from her love for God and for her neighbors, with her whole heart and a great deal of understanding and patience. This series of books has emerged from the many divine-spiritual teaching hours and conversations with the prophetess of God, Gabriele, for all those who want to learn for their life—and for the New Era, which has already been initiated.

Many a one already feels that a change is taking place, indeed, must take place, because even though negativity is currently still running riot, this world, as it is—with all the egocentric excesses in state, economy, religion and society—is subject to the law of cause and effect and is therefore in the process of passing away.

Very gradually the New Era is dawning, the Messianic, Sophianic Age of peacefulness, with people who make the law of love for God and neighbor the basis of their life, without religions and religious administrators. They are people of the Free Spirit—God in us and we in God.

Gabriele Publishing House—The Word

*From the Love, therefore,
came the Wisdom
and dwells among the people,
so that they may receive what God,
the Love and Wisdom,
has to say to them—
today in the great time
of liberation
of the generations
from a life
of restriction and affliction.*

(from the Christ-Revelation
"This Is My Word – Alpha and Omega")

God Can Be Found

*From a teaching hour with Gabriele
on March 9, 1997*

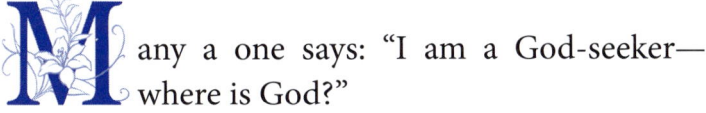any a one says: "I am a God-seeker—where is God?"

To seek God means to seek God in our inner being, because every person is the temple of God and God dwells in us. It is also written, "Seek and you will find." True God-seekers are also sought by God. This means that those who truly seek God strive to gradually realize what God wants.

What does God want from His children? He wants His children to keep His commandments step by step. God takes several steps toward the one who recognizes a small commandment of God and tries to take that step, that is, to fulfill this commandment.

We humans have the habit of looking for God somewhere or other—but He is always with us, He is always in us.

The one who truly seeks God will find Him. If we seek God, then we should enter our inner being aware that God is in us, and God can be found with every step we take toward God in us, by fulfilling the smallest commandment, for example, making peace with our neighbor and keeping peace. We then feel His nearness, because we become more peaceful, more insightful, more understanding, calmer. This is the nearness of God; with this He has already come a few steps toward us.

The Kingdom of God is in us, and each one of us has the key to the inner kingdom—it is Christ, it is the Redeemer-power in us and ultimately, also the teaching of the Sermon on the Mount. If we fulfill particles—I deliberately emphasize "particles"—of the Sermon on the Mount, then we gain the key: Christ in us. With this key, we gradually open the inner kingdom, the Kingdom of God, and we find entry. We will then realize that God is love. We will realize that God loves us, every one of us, even the greatest sinner. He loves us. We will then also feel: God is stillness—because we become calmer, because we make peace with our neighbor and are more understanding.

In this way, the God-seeker experiences God. He will never get to know God completely, because God is all-encompassing and powerful: He is in all the forces of the Being, in the kingdoms of nature, in the atom, God is everywhere—but we may recognize Him in the smallest steps we take toward God in us.

The smallest steps are, as stated, particles of the principles of the law. If we fulfill them, not only by resolving to do what God wants us to do, but by fulfilling these particles, these small principles, day by day, then we grow and mature into our inner being and open the inner kingdom with the help of our Redeemer, Christ. Then we feel that we can suddenly take bigger steps. We fulfill His commandments more and more and feel taken into an infinite love that we may feel, but which we can never get to know completely as long as we are human beings. We may recognize and feel it, and that should be our help and direction.

The one who believes that God exists commits himself, as it were, to take the path within. Such a person no longer complicates his life with many theories and phrases about how he may have found God, what possibilities he has exhausted, how he has fulfilled the laws of God—he does it because he feels the nearness of God, the help of the Christ of God. And he knows: The smallest step leads to the big step, to God. And he feels: One small step taken—and God comes several steps toward him.

Let us not see God as something that is far from us, that punishes us, that chastises us. We people punish and chastise ourselves through our sins, which are causes and come back to us as effects. But God loves us, He loves the greatest sinner.

If we listen a little more to our conscience, then, when we want to sin, we feel how the love, God, knocks at the inner gate—it is our conscience that is saying to us: "Change your thinking, do not think against your neighbor like that! Do not speak against your neighbor like that! Change your thinking—God is in your neighbor, just as He is in you. Change your thinking and begin to understand your neighbor. Change your thinking, forgive him for what he has done to you, and ask forgiveness from your neighbor as well. Do this!"—This is the subtle, gentle conscience; these are impulses from the innermost being, from the Kingdom of God; it is the divine in us that always admonishes us, but never forces us or even urges us to do anything. It speaks to us, and if we turn back, if we make peace with our neighbor, we notice how our consciousness expands and God draws closer to us. "Seek and you will find!" God can be found, not in the external world, not here and there, not in magnificent churches, but simply in ourselves.

And if we are agitated, if we are driven—nature shows us the calmness, in it there is growth; it is, again, God. Nature wants to help us so that we also blossom in God, mature through God, in order to then return home to the Kingdom of God then, when it is the last day in this earthly existence. May the last day of our earthly existence be, as it were, the first day in the Kingdom of God!

It is God's great love and His mighty humility that He responds to all His children. Even if the child takes only the smallest step—He responds to His child, for He loves it and wants to have it totally with Him again.

We know that our life is a storm and surge, an up and down, but if we do not allow the many all-too-many human aspects, the sinful aspects, and turn to God asking for support and for help, then we become calmer. This storm, this surge of life, gradually ebbs away, and we experience what calmness means.

Calmness means: For a start, we can think about something, about what preoccupies us, to figure out why this or that absorbs us so much, and whether this is God's will. Just by getting a little quiet to think about whether what we are thinking and doing is God's will, we already notice the help in our hearts. A small touch of insight, "O God, help me!"—a hint, so that we can fathom in depth our thoughts, our wanting, and we will find what moves us so much. If we clear it up with the help of our Redeemer, we will feel what calmnesss means.

Calmness also means being balanced, because with the conscious mind we weigh what is moving us, so as to clear it up. Either we then get it from our subconscious to resolve it with the help of the Christ of God, to transform it, as it were, or we do not allow at all in our conscious mind what the subconscious wants. If we do this, our consciousness expands; we become calmer; we turn inward.

God is the stillness. Before stillness, there is calm—to become calmer, in order to enter the stillness. This succeeds only when we look into the surge of our life to clear up this and that, so that the storm of sins can subside.

The true God-seeker perseveres in finding God! Even in the high waves of all-too-humanness, when he wants to give up, someone comes to him, and through their eyes, God looks at him and says: "Don't give up, persevere, you will find Me!"—and the one who perseveres wins.

We human beings complicate our life on Earth so much because sin is complicated. The greater our potential for sin, the more complicated we are. But at some point, we have to take the first step and say, "If I believe there is a God, then I have to get started!" Mostly, we then want to take a big step, and then we fail.

Dear fellow people, the smallest step is rewarded by God! And precisely the smallest step is decisive, so we can take bigger steps. Let us think of a small child—until it can straighten up, until it stands. One small step, and it feels joy and it also feels the reward from its parents; the parents rejoice. And how much more does God, our eternal Father, rejoice over the smallest step we take?

God gave His children absolute free will. Free will is the law in God's great love. God gave His children the pure, infinity as heritage. And the pure beings live in the heritage; they fulfill God's heritage: They fulfill the law of love, of freedom, of unity, of togetherness. God is the Spirit of evolution. He creates out of Himself ever more worlds, spiritual suns, spiritual beings, but they are all embedded in the great heritage. Each one has the same amount, namely, the whole.

The Free Spirit, God, has, of course, also given us freedom, because we were also pure beings in the Eternal Being, free in God. And in the Eternal Being, the freedom in God causes every spirit being in God to be creative, by feeling and acting according to the laws of the inner life, according to the laws of the Spirit of God. We human beings are children of God, even if we wear the sinful aspects around us—it is the "cloak," it is the human being who created himself with wrong thinking, that is, from the intellect, from the wrong thinking that is against God.

God will never take away our freedom. He will not simply take the negative, the all-too-human aspects away from us or prevent them, but rather, we have to recognize them ourselves through the law of freedom. And anyone who recognizes them will turn back and try to draw closer to God—and he will draw closer to God, too. And as he draws closer to God, he will never affirm or allow what is happening in the world.

Even if things are ever so haywire in this world: Christ is the victor, but not by force, not by fighting, but by approaching the individual—Christ in us—knocking at the door of the individual and saying, "Let today become your first day in Me! No longer do what you have recognized as sinful. Repent and clear it up, and fulfill the commandments step by step, then you will know who you ultimately are: a child of God with the fine feeling of the soul, through which God then speaks to the human being and acts through the human being."

What Is True Happiness?

*From a teaching hour with Gabriele
on January 20, 2008*

Many people say, "I do or do not do as I want, and in this way, I am free."—If that were so, all people who say that should be happy. But why are the fewest of people happy, and much less those who say, "I am free to do or not do whatever I want"?

Where does unhappiness come from in our society? Where do the disappointment and ties to people, to money and to goods come from? It is only because we humans do not make use of the days and always crave for more. The self-interest grows ever larger and cuts capers because we hear on radio and television: The gap between rich and poor is widening ever more. But even the rich are not happy. Why? Because rarely does a person—rich or poor or middle class, as we say—make use of the days. Many people, indeed, most of them, live through the day, make plans for the future and work toward owning this or that in the future, toward moving up the ladder of success in the future, toward savoring the so-called attractions of life in the future, and much more. As a result, the day is not used.

What we think on the days we don't use comes back; the inputs we made that day come back. We don't even know what we have input, because we are constantly working toward the future. As a result, we don't even feel and sense who we are. We want something that may not even be in our genes. We want to take up a certain occupation, to climb higher on the ladder of success. Perhaps, however, that is not in our genetic material; perhaps the soul did not bring it along with it. But we crave this and forget that we also live today, on this day, and that this day is our day, which wants to reflect various things to us.

The day comes into our thoughts, into our world of ideas, into our desires and into our passions. Where do the desires go? They mostly go to our neighbors. This means that we have expectations of our fellow people, for example, that certain people contribute or do for us what we expect. If they don't do it, then we are not only disappointed, but we disparage them, judge them, berate them. All these thoughts, all these unseemly tendencies shape our days to come.

This day, on which we are disappointed, is passed on to the coming days. And all that we feel, think, speak and do today will come back to us on another day. Therefore, we ourselves are often the brakes for our future—today we put the brakes on what we might want tomorrow.

Through our expectations we create dependencies. Ultimately, we are dependent on our neighbor, who is supposed to do or even does do something for us. We, in turn, obligate ourselves to this person to do something for him, so that he does for us what we want. We use nice words; we make a gesture with flowers or a small gift—but with the ulterior motive that he continue to do this or that for us. If he does not, we are again disappointed. And this disappointment turns into hostility, and even into a quarrel.

Here, I am thinking of marriage and partnership. It is precisely in marriage and partnership that these bindings arise. We expect our partner to do this or that for us. We expect our partner to praise us, to find us beautiful, for example, as a woman, and much more. If our partner does not behave in this way, because he is thinking about other things or because he has company or business worries, then we are disappointed. This disappointment again works against the partner. Another time something similar happens: The partner from whom we expect something does not do it. Doubts arise, unkind words are spoken, quarrels, even hostility, come up in marriage and partnership. The person who is disappointed says to herself, "I'll get even with him! If *he* ever wants something from me, I won't do anything for him either." This is how the mutual bindings, the mistrust, the hostility are formed. The mistrust and the hostility possibly lead to quarrels, even to hatred, and then to separation.

It is quite another thing when we ask our neighbor to do something: "Could you please do this for me?" However, we should make this request only when we cannot do ourselves what we are asking for, whatever the reason. If our partner fulfills our request, then we feel that he has been accommodating. We can then also give thanks, and a link is formed.

Therefore, to ask is not to demand, but to ask, because we are momentarily unable to do something ourselves. From this comes a "thank you" and a certain joy, which turns into trust.

In every binding there are doubts regarding the other person, especially in marriage and partnership. But in trust there is togetherness and cooperation. The churches say that peace should develop from marriage. How, then? Only by keeping what Jesus of Nazareth said, *"Do to others as you would have them do to you!"* In other words, "Do not do to others what you do not want done to you!"

When we demand something from another person that we could do ourselves, and our neighbor does not do it for us, then discord arises. That is how it is in marriage, that is how it is in everyday life, at work, in society, among friends—everywhere. But if we can't fulfill something because we can't do it at the moment, and we ask our neighbor to do it, then that is something entirely different, and that leads to friendship, that leads to peace, that leads to togetherness. Everything else is insincere; everything else leads to dependence, to quarrel, to unhappiness, to discord.

Let us also think about the desire for recognition. What does it mean? We expect. And we bind ourselves to the ones who praise us; we always want more from them. Why can't we reflect on ourselves? We give away our mental and physical qualities by constantly binding ourselves to others, by expecting something from them.

Happiness means that we are not only true to ourselves, to ourselves as a person, but also to what Jesus of Nazareth taught us, because Jesus, the Christ, taught us independence, which makes us free.

What is often the cause of unfreedom?—Because many are dissatisfied with themselves. What gives rise to being bound to another person? By expecting from them what we don't have. We need recognition; we need praise; we need the word "merit" from others. If we don't get it, then we feel unhappy; we feel inferior, then we are discontented, in short: totally dissatisfied, even frustrated.—Why? Because we always look to others to enhance us.

As long as we do that, we will never be free. Today I am more convinced than ever that freedom develops only from ourselves, from each one of us. Everyone should take a good look at himself and, for a start, also look at himself in the mirror. The one who wants to become free should analyze his thoughts, his feelings, his desires, his passions in the question: "Do they correspond to me? Or am I just expecting something from this?" If for no other reason a person dresses with others in mind, he is disguising himself. Thus, he does not dress according to his mentality, not according to his nature—he dresses to please others. Here we have the addiction to please. If the addiction to please is not reciprocated, then the person is totally depressed. And so we experience the disguise, which occasionally seems like a theatrical performance. One dresses differently; one presents oneself differently, to receive praise, recognition and appreciation.

If we don't do that, but go back to our basis and make sure that we are somewhat satisfied with ourselves, then our consciousness expands and we also become more charitable toward our neighbor. The prerequisite is, of course, that we make use of the days and look at our life situation, that we do not develop egocentricity in desires, in passions for the time to come—for example, money, goods and much more. If we do that, we will neither live nor use our days, but will yearn for the future—and the future will certainly not bring us what we desire. Because what we have previously input, that is what comes to us in the future.

And should a poor person become rich someday, then the question arises as to whether he is happy with the wealth he desired from his youth on. Maybe for a short time, then he is unhappy again.— Why? Because the days he didn't make use of come back to him as a rich man and make him unhappy. Then he may say, "I have not made use of my youth, I have not made use of my whole life, what good is wealth to me?" That is the downward spiral.

The life cycle upward always has to begin with ourselves. The discontent is in ourselves—we want something from our neighbor. Why can't we be satisfied, first of all, with the way we presently are, with the way life created us? What we have, what we have made of our life, what we are satisfied with, that makes us happy. But the craving for others to make us happy, always leads downward.

Therefore, this means that we have to find the way to ourselves, first to ourselves as a human being and then beyond that to the inner values. Both, the human being and the inner values, form the character that makes us free, because we no longer disparage others, because we expect nothing from others, because we have grown out of ourselves, out of our inner being, and do not lose face when we ask for help, because we cannot do this or that at the moment.

We can be honest with each other because the one who is free expects nothing from others—and through this he is also honest. He can also honestly admit his weaknesses and say, "Here, these are my weaknesses." But he does not demand that others cover up his weaknesses by praising him and much more.

To make the best of each day means to input our evolution, to indeed create a perspective for the future, but not to crave its fulfillment, but to strive for it every day, step by step. However, to make the best of each day also means to make the best for ourselves, to find our way to ourselves.

We come from the Eternal Kingdom, from the Kingdom of God, and are incarnated. That is why Jesus, the Christ, came to us and brought us the laws of life, of the Kingdom of God. We read them in the Sermon on the Mount as well as in the Ten Commandments that God gave through Moses.

"Do to others what you would have them do to you," spoken differently: "Do not do to others what you do not want to have done to you"—these sentences are life's wisdom, which lead to a quality of life and let us live with our fellow people. Whether in the family, whether in partnership, in our field of work, our circle of friends, wherever we may be—we have to learn to find ourselves.

And when we are discontent, we ought to actually ask ourselves: "With what am I dissatisfied?" This "With what am I dissatisfied?" contains in turn: Make the best of it!

"I am dissatisfied with myself"—well, with what? Make the best of it! Each day is a help to make the best out of each day, and ultimately, also the best for us. And thus, we gradually find our way out of the tangle of bindings, expectations, dissatisfaction, dependency, hostility, disappointment and much more. Make the most of yourself, of your life, every day. No matter where you are, practice and always remember the words of Jesus of Nazareth: *"Whatever you want others to do for you, you do it first."* We expect nothing of others—we expect everything of ourselves!

If we are free, rooted in the teachings of Jesus, the Christ, then we will never live in want—that is certain. We will not have lavish wealth, nor will we strive for power and prestige—we are modest. And in the modesty that is rooted in ourselves lies freedom—and freedom makes us happy.

I have a very simple recipe: I am always happy when I can make someone else happy. Being happy means not to bind ourself to our neighbor. Make the other person happy with good thoughts, with some honest, trusting words, with the appropriate help—just as I am able to help, in prayer, which I also fulfill myself. Then these thoughts will also reach the people who are open for them, and I have thus made them a little bit happy. That is what brings me the most happiness.

The Speaking God

From a teaching hour with Gabriele
on May 29, 2009

God, the Eternal, is the eternally revealing Spirit. Unceasingly, God speaks in our heart at every moment. God, our Father, taught us in His commandments: *"You shall have no other gods before me."* We human beings have acquired so many "idols" that we have distanced ourselves from the All-One, the eternal God, the speaking God.

Our gods are called: denigration, aggrandizement, egocentric behavior with the "mine" and "me." For many people the neighbor is a stranger, although in the depth of their soul he is their brother, their sister from the Kingdom of God. Greed, envy, resentment, hostility, enmity, belligerent behavior toward the neighbor in thoughts and words are some of these "gods" that are alien to God. For many of us, they are the "gods" we worship, to whom we subjugate ourselves, and they talk us into turning to them more and more. They talk and talk and lead us into the shadows of existence, so that we hardly realize anymore that the speaking God is omnipresent and that He speaks in us—in every tree, in every plant, in every bush, in every little animal—He speaks in the mighty stars and planets of the All, the universe.

God, the All-Law, is all-effective everywhere, also in the sphere of matter. We realize that the speaking God is the Spirit of love, the Spirit of omnipresence, the eternally speaking Spirit of our eternal Father.

We people often need an image to be able to understand that when we turn away from God, we no longer hear God, our eternal Father, and Christ, our Redeemer. We expose ourselves to the shadows of the "gods."

How is it when our continent turns away from the sun? Then it is dark for us—but the sun shines constantly! It is similar in our existence that is rich in shadows. God, the eternal light, shines omnipresently and radiates in us. And every divine ray of love is the word of love to us. However, if we lead a shadowy existence, how can we receive the sun, the light, the love, the word of the Eternal?

If a continent were to be without the light of the sun for a long, long time, without the warming rays of the sun, there would be mold on the continent; vegetation could no longer exist. Every flower would bend; every shrub would drop its leaves. No tree could bear fruit anymore. It is the darkness.

It is similar for many people in the body. The soul has darkened because the person has turned away from God. In the soul is the source of light, the word of God, the eternal speaking Spirit. But our body cells are vegetating. We complain about sickness, about hardship, suffering, about our fate. We stand in the darkness, turned away from God's light. The darkness gains ground. It is like a continent that no longer turns toward the sun.

No matter which language we human beings speak—God does not have the language of people, but He radiates into our thoughts, into our words and wants to tell us something. What?

The first thing that He could say to us is, "I Am your Lord and God. You shall have no other gods before me."

And the second thing He could say to us, "See, I have given you the Ten Commandments through Moses—live accordingly!"

And the third thing that He wants to say to us, "Oh see, My child, you have not been left alone! I have sent My Son to the Earth, the Co-Regent of the heavens. Jesus of Nazareth, the Christ of God, became your Redeemer. He is the power and the light from and in Me. He is in Me and I in Him. It is the Spirit of the Christ of God. He speaks in you, in each one of you. Pay attention to the teachings of My Son," the Lord would say to us, "and you will turn to the speaking God, the Christ of God, and receive the light, the word, the help, the love, the warmth, the security and the protection."

Many call themselves Original Christians. And many an Original Christian, but also many another one—whether he calls himself Christian, Moslem, Hindu, or an Atheist—can sense the word of love, the speaking God, who points out to us, for example, that now and today we should keep the commandments.

To each of us are given the teachings of the Christ, in which He shows us again and again, including now and today, through our conscience, that we should develop remorse for the sin we become aware of, clear it up and no longer do it. We feel it in the subtle stirrings of our heart.

All these are impulses of love; it is the speaking God. In this way, He wants us to come into harmony with Him and with our innermost, eternal being that comes from Him. He wants us to be deeply linked with ourselves and with Him, indeed, that we are one.

Perhaps a beautiful flower suddenly catches our eye, a rose, a carnation, a daffodil—its fragrance is the word of love; it is the fragrance of the homeland; it is the speaking God who shows us that in everything there is life. Life is communication, and communication is the language of love.

If the language of love rises in our hearts, our prayers gain vitality and truthfulness. They are then no longer mere words, but the direct sensations of the heart to the great Spirit who is so near to each one of us. We are then truly no longer lonely and alone. Then we feel the warmth and goodness of God in us, His comfort and care.

All people, no matter of what faith they are, are embedded in the great love, in the light. But often we do not want to perceive this. Why not? Because we have not yet grasped that there is more than what our earthly life presents to us.

For how long do we still want to love the shadows or accept their existence? For how long do we still want to occupy ourselves with our "gods"? We then feel like strangers. Why? Because the gods are alien to God. We ourselves have created them, and we should dissolve them. Then we will turn more and more to the light, like the continent to the sun. Then the dawn awakens in us—dawn is breaking, the light is rising, and we feel: God is present, at every moment.

That was a message of the heart that is spoken to all of us, whether Original Christian, Christian, Moslem, Hindu, Buddhist or Atheist. Because all, every one, bear within the speaking God.

How beautiful nature is! Let us think about our walks. Do we go through nature with our "gods"?—

Or do we walk at the hand of the Christ of God, who wants to awaken in our heart more and more the fine inner sensation that the Christ of God is the speaking God?

Let us turn to Christ in us. He will never close Himself off from us, but will come toward us. For it is written: *"Ask, and it will be given to you; seek, and you will find; knock, and it will be opened to you. For the one who asks receives; the one who seeks finds; and the one who knocks will have it opened to him."*

Let us experience Christ in us! Then we will also experience God, our Father, as the creative power in every step we take. Particularly when we take a relaxing walk, we can, if we open ourselves to Him, sense and fathom that God is present.

This is what we desire for all of us: to feel the present power. Only then, do we feel taken into the love, into the fullness of the Spirit, into the speaking God. And we realize: We are not alone. God, our Father, is present in us, and Christ, our Redeemer, is active in the Spirit of the Father. We are secure, enveloped in a powerful light. It is the moment in God's omnipresence.

And to grasp and experience this in the various situations of our everyday life gives our life meaning and substance. It opens up a dimension of life that seemed closed to us before.

Keep the Inner Calm in Every Situation

From a teaching hour with Gabriele on November 26, 1995

God is a near God. Many of us are still influenced by a distant God. Many of us think we have to pray to heaven in order to eventually reach God. But God can be reached only in us. Only once we have reached Him in ourselves do we establish communication with all things, for God is in all forms of life.

"Keep the inner calm in every situation" also means to become aware that God is near to each one of us.

Let us keep this awareness in our hearts: God is very near to us; God is our conversation partner. God, the love, God, our Father, the Spirit of love in us, knows us; He knows about our "pros and cons." Let us keep in our hearts that we may speak with Him; let us keep in our hearts that He loves us and never punishes us, that everything that comes to us in the way of negativity—blows of fate, worries and the like—are our own inputs, the inputs of hatred, of envy, of destruction.

But in His law, God has neither hatred nor envy nor destruction. God is always unchanged, the helping and giving love; He is the Father with whom we can talk. Even if we say: "We do not hear Him," we have to admit that we want to hear Him in the way that *we* want it. But God reveals Himself to each one of us. He reveals Himself not only through the words of the *"I Am,"* but He reveals Himself in the situations that come toward us. God reveals Himself to us in daily occurrences.

It's usually the case that when a disagreeable situation comes our way, our blood begins to boil; we get all worked up. What does this mean? "I'm right! I want to solve the situation as I think is right!" Then we cannot hear God.

God is just, because in every disagreeable situation that causes us to seethe, we are involved in something negative. I deliberately say "involved," because our neighbors, who are part of this situation, may also be involved. But if we say: "I'll solve the situation as I want!" or: "Let the others solve the situation!"—then we are agitated; we do not let God prevail. But God is in every situation; God is the help. And in everything negative that we have contributed to, so that things are the way they presently are, God is, again, the help.

That God gives us an answer in the situation, that God solves the situation for us—this first requires the step of belief. Do we believe in the near God? Do we believe that He is able to help us out of any situation? Do we believe that He is our Father? Do we believe that we are His children? Do we believe that He loves us? Do we believe that He helps us—not only by telling us how we should do it, but that He is just and wants to help everyone involved in the situation?

If our faith is bigger than a mustard seed, we begin to trust. And when at one point, our blood boils, then we say: "Lord, you are the stillness! I know that I am involved here; I am also to blame in this situation. I will clear up my guilt, my part, but You, You help us all to resolve this situation according to Your holy law of love and justice."

If we can say this full of confidence in our heart, then it suddenly gets warm in us. We get calmer. Our turbulent mind calms down, and an inkling comes up in us—an inkling of what we can contribute toward the solution of the situation. We suddenly gain inner calm. Our senses turn inward. Our sense of hearing suddenly becomes quite calm and, in this calmness, very alert, we hear what our neighbor is saying. From what the neighbor says, we may discern an aspect of the solution—it is God's answer through our neighbor. Again with another, we suddenly hear from the conversation aspects that concern us, and we realize: This is our sinfulness, our guilt in this situation. We then feel in our heart that we are getting calmer and calmer, because the solution is developing—for us personally and for the situation.

Thus, to stay calm in the situation means to first of all ask ourselves: Do we believe? Do we entrust ourselves to Him, God, or do we want Him to resolve things as we want? Who knows us better? Does our neighbor know us? Our neighbor does not know us. Not even we know ourselves down to the root of the evil. But God knows us. And when we realize that He does not punish us for our sinfulness, but wants to help us—to help us out of the situation, to recognize our sinful part and to clear it up—then we gain confidence in the awareness: Only He can be relied upon; He alone can be relied upon.

If we can hold onto that, that we can rely solely on Him—well, where do we go then? Solely to Him! Unless we want something from people. Then we go to people. And people always share their all-too-human aspects, their ego-self. If we are satisfied with that, then we will never do justice to the situation, and thus, solve it according to God's will, but will create more negative situations yet again.

Therefore: To keep calm in the situation also means to question ourselves: How do I relate to God, my Father, and to Christ, my Redeemer?

It is about becoming aware, becoming aware every day—and that, over and over again: "He is a near God"—the realization that we should keep in our hearts: "God loves us; God knows us; we can rely on Him. He resolves the situation with us and through us and through all people in a just way, so that we do not create any more difficulties."

When we become aware of this and when, over the course of time, we go into our inner being and realize that it is of no use at all to rely on our ego, nor on the ego of our neighbor—because it only confuses us and always brings more difficulties—then we surrender to Him. But surrendering to Him means, in turn: "The way You solve the situation, the way You work through me, is just!"

And the justice of God is usually different from what we want, from our dogmatism. These are, namely, our problems and difficulties. The ego always puts itself above God; it always wants to be right. As long as we want to be right, *we* want to solve the situation and again create difficulties from it. This is the restlessness of our mind, and through this, we will never find the calm and never find the way to God, and will never see God's justice prevail, or hear God's justice prevail.

"Keep the inner calm in every situation." Once we apply this statement to our thoughts or to our world of feelings, we will know why we cannot keep calm in a situation.

Then, when a situation needs to be dealt with, we should not wait for long—we should immediately look for the solution. If we can't clear up something right away, it can help to say again and again: "Father, not my will is done, but Yours. You know the solution, and in due time, I will know the solution." If this comes from the heart, then we immediately feel stirrings in our inner being, and we know how we can contribute to the solution. But again and again, what is important is the surrender and the dedication to God: "Father, not my will be done, but Yours!"

The call to within, "Please help me!" is the turning to Him. The child surrenders now, in this moment of the situation. We become calmer, and the answer is to recognize our part, to recognize what we should clear up and no longer do. And the moment we firmly resolve not to do that anymore, we feel this wonderful liberation; it is a feeling of the inner being that is indescribable when God also answers us in this way.

We could also say that it is a conversation with the Lord. We pray, and the answer or the solution comes. It doesn't necessarily have to rise from our heart; we suddenly have it in a feeling, or we see a picture, or someone else says, look here or there! The answers are many and varied—they are conversations with the Lord.

Our topic is: "Keep the inner calm in every situation." What might we take from this, for example, for the coming week, indeed, for the rest of our lives?—"Seek a dialogue with God." That does not mean we should listen in—please, we should not do that!—but it means to entrust ourselves to God. Let us begin to ask ourselves: Do we believe? Do we trust Him? Can we surrender to Him? In prayer, in deep prayer, in the call for help, in the devotion of the heart, we find the dialogue with God. He often does not answer us in the word from the heart, but He answers us, as stated, through our neighbor, in the situation. We suddenly get a warm feeling, an image rises—and much, much more.

God speaks to us through many mouths. Let us keep this awareness: God speaks to us, but His love and justice want it differently than we want, than the ego wants, therefore: the surrender.

We Greet Spring.
We bear within everything that lives.
Everything that lives radiates to us and speaks to us

From a teaching hour with Gabriele
on April 8, 1988

The one who wanders more and more to within, to the "kingdom in us," also feels that the homeland, the eternal light, is ever closer—and he will increasingly let go of his human thoughts and no longer take himself so seriously.

The moment we no longer take ourselves so seriously, life awakens in us and around us, and we will experience the wonders of life anew each day.

Why are we all placed in spring? Just as we are placed in the day anew each day, we have again been placed in this season. Have we ever thought about why? Nothing happens by chance. Why do we experience spring in the Earth's garment this year?

Doesn't spring also want to tell us something?

If we walk through nature with alert senses, we find out what spring wants to tell us. On the whole, it wants to tell us, "See, just as everything sprouts from the soil, the life, so do I, the Spirit, the life, want to grow out of you for My glorification."

When we look at the flowers, the plants, we see that nothing grows from the outside. The soil needs sun, rain and wind for growth, that means the plants, the bushes, trees and flowers need sun, rain and wind. But nothing grows from the outside—everything sprouts from the soil and shows itself in the beautiful colors and forms. It is similar with us. We, too, need the light of the inner being, and, figuratively speaking, the "clouds," in order to recognize the shadows of our soul. If we have eliminated the clouds of our ego, then the sun shines from within, and we shine all the more.

Why does spring come, why summer, why autumn and winter? Because in spring the planet turns toward the sun. The radiation becomes stronger, the sunlight more intense; it penetrates the soil and out of the soil comes the diversity of life.

Totally different flowers come in summer; we also see the fruits, how they ripen. We experience autumn totally differently—likewise the diversity and form of the leaves, the colors, the exterior. But everything comes "from within," everything is the life from God.

This is how we want to include spring in our lives. Only once we approach the inner light does it begin to sprout and grow in us. What then grows out of us? The positive forces. The human aspects disappear; the high ethics and morals, the inner life, become active, and we are similar to the flower: We radiate what is given to us from within, light and strength.

When we look at the flowers and plants, we can be sure that everything shines on us and illuminates us. And everything that shines on us also communicates with us. Those who believe that the flowers, the bushes, the trees, all life are mute have not yet developed life in themselves. When we see the diversity of the flowers and the plants, the branches, we may say: Every single flower communicates with us. How is this possible? The various flowers belong to a collective, and this great collective is in the soul of the Earth and radiates the spiritual life to the roots, to everything that is in the soil and bears life. Plants, flowers, shrubs, trees, animals, even stones communicate with us. It is the collective of stones, the collective of plants, flowers, shrubs, that communicate to us. We experience the language of nature and the language of the animals not outside of us, but in our inner being, in our spiritual body, because the essence of all collectives, of all life forms is there.

We bear within us everything that lives. If we as human beings have gained access to these collectives, that is, if there are no dense shadows over them, that is, burdens, then we sense in our inner being that everything that lives radiates to us and speaks to us, that is, communicates with us. We rejoice in the chirping of birds. If we listen carefully, we perceive that the birds are talking to each other. And if we have accessed the powers of the birds, the life, this consciousness of the birds, then we hear within us what they are saying to each other.

The stones speak. We are deaf as long as we think only of ourselves and believe that we are merely human beings made of flesh and bone, water and earth. If we were merely human beings, then we would have hardly any relationship to the life around us, because we would not possess this diversity within us. But our spiritual body is made up of all these life forms, and thus, within us is the spiritual body that bears in itself all these collectives; for all that we see is law and thus life. The moment our human shadows depart from our spirit body, via waves of sensation we feel: Nature communicates. Every little animal, no matter how inconspicuous, is part of a collective, as long as it does not have a part-soul yet. And this collective, in turn, communicates with us. We do not hear it externally, but we hear it in our spiritual body. The stones radiate, they live, and what lives communicates with us. The stars radiate, and the essence of the stars communicates with us.

The Christ of God said in His revelation, *"Take up your heritage."* What does He want to tell us with this? "Step into life, develop the life I have given you, all of creation as essence." This essence is our spiritual body. Thus we are not only human beings, but we consist of spirit, soul and physical body—and ultimately, we are infinitely rich, for all life forms want to serve and please us. Neither plants nor stones, neither the radiation of the stars nor the animals want us any harm—they want to serve us. When we say, "Many animals attack," we should feel far, far back into the past. Have not we ourselves become fighters against nature? And many animals that possess a part-soul absorb our combative negative vibrations. They are afraid of us and then they attack.

So let us put aside our combative mood, our human ego, let us become again what is given to us—the life from God's life—then we will experience infinity in us, and no flower, no bush, no tree, no stone, no animal is foreign to us; it is a part of ourselves.

They all belong to various collectives, but the collectives radiate to us. If the spiritual collective is developed in us, then we feel what they want to tell us—even if we are not able to translate it into our language—and we feel within ourselves that they are flowing love, forces of light and goodwill toward us.

Let us practice sensing the life that is ultimately also in us.

Each one of us could take a flower or a plant. We behold it, that is, we don't look at it—when we look at it, we perceive the outer details. "To behold" means we take in the whole impression, draw all the radiant substance inward, immerse ourselves in our inner being, and sense—well, what do we sense?

Let us practice this!

Life gives strength. Strength flows to us from everything, if only we are able to absorb it. At the moment when we are only somewhat free and our human thoughts no longer block us, we feel the life.

Some people think: "We need herbs and plants for our body, they do us good. We like to drink teas made from herbs and plants"; so for us, it is a matter of course to drink herbal tea, for example.

We believe that a little herb is good for our organism only once we have picked it and use it, for example, as tea or seasoning. Yes, that is certainly good; we need the tea and the seasoning. But whether a little herb remains in the ground or we use it as tea—it radiates and gives itself to us. The same life radiates to us, whether we meet it at the wayside or in the woods, on the field, in the garden. It radiates and wants to radiate to us the forces that our organism needs. The soul bears these life energies in itself, and if they are active in the soul, then they also radiate into the body.

Thus, nature is given to us so that we not only enjoy it, but also absorb its forces, and we can do that by not only using it as tea, as seasoning and the like, but also by absorbing it in the way that nature, the life, gives itself to us.

What is it like when we suddenly realize: Everything lives—and everything that lives feels? Then it will no longer be possible for us to deliberately trample a plant. Unknowingly, it happens all the time, but with this unawareness, it is as if the Creator were to say, "You have a material body; I sacrifice Myself for you and form a carpet for you." However, when we deliberately trample life, we shadow the collective in our inner being.

The same happens with regard to animals, when we deliberately kill animals, when we torture and slaughter them and much more—we burden our soul, because everything feels. The animal also feels, and when we consciously kill an animal or have it slaughtered, then we burden ourselves, and the relationship to the life of nature, to the animals, becomes more and more restricted. The person becomes ever coarser, desecrates nature and desecrates the Earth. In the moment the inner life awakens in a person, he will appreciate the life of the Earth, because it is a part of him.

Each day, we should rejoice in budding nature and at the same time realize that just as a leaf unfolds from its sheath, we too should unfold from the capsule of the human ego, bursting it, as it were, in the awareness that we are children of God and children of divine love.

Birds, too, and not only birds, speak by singing and thus express what corresponds to their consciousness. All animals radiate life and share themselves with us. If we merely look at the animals, we will judge them. We say, "That's a dog, that's a cat, that's a hedgehog, that's a frog, that's a toad, that's a beetle" and much more.

But when we look the animal in the eye and take in its overall radiation, many of us feel that the animal is speaking to us. Whether it's horses, whether it's cows, whether it's sheep—let's look them in the eye! The eyes radiate what they want to convey to us. It is wonderful to experience this once—to behold, not only to look and judge, but to behold and take in, then we experience that every animal feels. We will then gradually also sense the part-soul or the collective in us, because what radiates from the animal radiates into the spiritual collective in us, in our spirit body. If this collective in us is not overlaid with burdens, then we sense what the animal wants to tell us. We will then no longer heedlessly walk past our second neighbors, the animals, but when we encounter animals, we will ask: "What do they want to tell us now?" It it not by chance that we have met them, and it is not by chance that we become aware of a flower by the wayside; it is not by chance that we suddenly stand admiringly before a flowering shrub, and it is not by chance that we are drawn to the garden to look at the flowers and the shrubs. Nothing happens by chance—everything wants to tell us something, all these encounters, or that we are drawn to the garden, that we suddenly become aware of a certain shrub, and much more.

Life is rich, infinitely rich; it is the abundance—and we have this abundance in ourselves. We could never feel the life of an animal, a plant, if there were not the same thing in us, the magnet, which practically attracts the radiation of this plant, this animal, the stone, the radiation of the stars. If we awaken spiritually more and more, then we feel that God's light is everywhere, that the Father's Spirit dwells in us and His creative power in all forms of life.

We could also ask ourselves: What do flowers have to say? The collectives among themselves—collectives are various states of consciousness—exchange energies with each other and thus communicate.

Collectives are consciousness forces, and each plant species has, in turn, another consciousness; that is, it radiates according to its development.

Consciousness is development, ranges of consciousness are evolutionary stages. The various stones, for example, belong to a collective, depending on their composition. Therefore, there are many collectives of stones, of minerals. It is the same with the plants. The different plants belong to different collectives, and thus, they have different aspects of consciousness. The animals that do not have a part-soul yet also belong to a huge field of consciousness, so we could also call this a collective. From this respective collective stones, plants and animals are then supplied with spirit power—except for the animals with part-souls, as these already possess an active core of being and receive as we do. With us, all seven basic powers are developed; in the part-souls of the animals, perhaps three or two, depending on how far the development of the part-soul has progressed.

Just as the spirit beings give joy to the Creator-God through their positive radiation, so do all life forms, including the stones. And if we can absorb this radiation, then the collective tells us exactly what is good for our life.

When we consciously walk through nature, we recharge our battery enormously, because the life around us gives itself to us. It is there to serve us in love. If we turn to the life in love, then this communication takes place, the flow of positive forces.

Take the Freedom.
Become Free—Be Free!

From a seminar of the same title with Gabriele
in 2003

Cosmic freedom is one of the divine principles active in the law of God, in the seven basic powers. Without love, there is no freedom and without freedom, there is no love.

Many a one will now think, "What does freedom have to do with love?"—and vice versa: "What does love have to do with freedom?"

Let the neighbor have his independence.
Give what you expect

Let us first shed light on the word "freedom." Where there is no freedom, there is unfreedom, bondage, in short, binding.

Thus, binding is in the way of our freedom. Let us therefore explore the question: What is binding, and how does it develop?

Binding grows out of self-love, which says, "Everything only for me!" We can "take" our freedom, that is, attain it, only if we truly love our neighbor, if we think of our neighbor with our heart, if we are well-disposed toward him and do not expect anything from him—on the contrary, we give to him. This is what Jesus, the Christ, called for in His Sermon on the Mount: Give what you expect. In other words: You should always first give what you expect from others. Then you will gradually forget your own ego, the person-centered, egotistical thinking that revolves around your own personal well-being.

Love is giving. Those who do not reject their neighbor, but learn to understand him and stand by him—even in many a situation that he does not understand and that is difficult to see through—can take the liberty to say, "I'll do what I can for you, but I won't let myself be bound." Of course, this presupposes that we, for our part, do not bind ourselves to our neighbor. To bind always means to hold on to our neighbor, to hang on to him, ultimately, to make him dependent on us as well. We then give just enough to make the other compliant.

Someone who realizes that he is bound might now think, "I want to shake off this binding. I want to gain freedom. So I will push my neighbor, to whom I am bound, away from me; I will distance myself from him, abandon him—either internally or even externally." But in this way, we do not overcome the binding. This is not freedom, but rather it is against freedom, because freedom is in equality and also in unity. And in unity there is always the responsibility toward our fellow human being.

Let us recognize the difference between to "abandon" and to "let go." To abandon means to turn our back on our neighbor, to let him down, to forsake him. If we abandon our neighbor, either internally or externally, we are shirking our responsibility and at the same time, abandoning unity.

God never turns away from His children. Why not? God is unity, and unity is love: selfless, impersonal, always giving. He expects nothing for Himself and leaves each of us free to make our own decisions and to develop ourselves. God says: "you shall," but He lets us go.

We should learn to no longer bind ourselves to our neighbor, to leave him his independence, to be independent ourselves, to let go of him, so that he can unfold, and we can unfold as well. Freedom develops from this.

Binding makes us unhappy

Why it is so important for us to let go of bindings and unfulfilled wishes? Because they make us unhappy.

Let us look around us: Many people are unhappy. If we question our own existence, we will very soon feel in ourselves that people who bind themselves to us or people to whom we bind ourselves cannot develop freely. From this it follows that those who bind themselves to others cannot develop freely.

Each of us strives for happiness; we want to be happy. Therefore, the question to ourselves is: Who makes us unhappy? Or: What makes us unhappy?

Many a one will now say, "I'm afraid to let go. It could be that I would then be alone." Anyone who lives in this fear has to recognize that he lives in bondage and not in freedom. Binding makes us unhappy.

We never feel forsaken when we do not bind others to us, and we do not bind ourselves to our fellow human beings. Those who hold on to their neighbor are self-centered, selfish, unloving, and every lack of love makes us unhappy. We then expect our happiness from others—they should make us happy. They should give to us from their energy; we do not want to give, but to take.

"Take the freedom"—the same as, gain freedom—that means, first of all, to make sure we know what true freedom means.

*Actively master your life—
question your moods and inhibitions*

How often do we hear, "I take the liberty to say or do this or that," which usually amounts to doing what we feel like doing, that is, what we want to do, more or less inconsiderately, without taking into account the latitude and concerns of our neighbor. What about freedom here? In reality, we harm ourselves and the other one, because the freedom we take for ourselves usually makes the other one ultimately unhappy. For many, taking one's freedom means living at the expense of the other.

If we analyze the word "freedom" and relate the analysis to ourselves, that is, question why we bind ourselves to our fellow people or allow others to bind themselves to us, we will realize that it is solely the selfish ego and the fear of possibly being rejected by others.

Many a person shrugs his shoulders in misfortune and says, "Well, that's just my fate." Those who are so resigned to fate do not believe in freedom. We have the freedom to determine our fate ourselves, to remedy the causes in time with the power of the Christ of God or to reduce or mitigate an effect that has already occurred, for instance, a blow of fate. It depends on us, on how we deal with the circumstances of our earthly existence—whether we truly live by actively managing it, or react passively, bound by fate.

Many people behave like slaves—slaves to their own human ego and consequently, subject to the influence of the ego of others. They bind themselves to their own weaknesses. Such people talk about freedom and do not know that freedom lies in thinking, speaking and acting. Every person determines for himself his development and thus his path. He has the freedom to decide at every moment.

No person is free from moods and inhibitions. But our moods and inhibitions, everything that touches us, are indications from our soul; the movements of our disposition are the language of our soul. It speaks to us and asks us to question the moods, the inhibitions and movements, in order to become free from what we have imposed and may continue to impose on it through our feelings, thoughts, words and actions.

Alertness toward ourselves is the order of the day. Before we put our personal, all-too-human "foot" in our mouths, that is, before we fall back into our old mistakes, our faulty attitudes and weaknesses, we will have already felt an uneasy feeling in our stomach area, which we had simply pushed aside. Thus, we may have gotten into situations that would not have been necessary if we had listened to this inner feeling, to the pointing finger of our conscience. That's why this is so important: As soon as we feel uncomfortable—be it inhibitions, disturbances, a certain uneasiness—we should pay attention: Stop! Here something is being signaled to me; here my subconscious is speaking; here my soul is speaking to me. What does it want to tell me today, indeed, at this moment?

Let's work it out and not be afraid to look at it closely—because these are certainly not always nice things—and if we are willing to become free of our bad traits, then we will feel what true freedom means. An inner strength develops and ultimately, also a feeling of goodwill toward our fellow people. We no longer expect anything from them. We can give them as much as we can, without binding ourselves to them or without their binding themselves to us.

The path to the fulfillment of the meaning of our existence on Earth leads to freedom, to being free. For we are on this Earth to free ourselves in good time from our all-too-humanness with the help of the Spirit of God in us, in order to then take the way of freedom—for our neighbor, without being dependent on him.

This is the path of the human being to the Kingdom of Heaven. Everything else is a selfish path, which many tread, over years, decades, to get rid of their ego, but which leads over and over again into this side of life. That is why there are so many people. On the other hand, the way of freedom is to be free, to be free in good time, and thus truly serve our neighbor. That is life. That is the following of Christ. This leads more and more to nearness to God, to being linked with God, as well as to inner security. This is the way for every human being—if they want to follow it.

Only self-recognition, the knowledge of the truth about ourselves, makes us free. It often takes a little courage to look at ourselves honestly, that is, ruthlessly, especially if we have failed to do so for years. Without being aware of it, our "ego claim" often hides behind excuses that begin with, for example, "I just want that ..." or "But the other person has ..." or "It's quite normal that ..." and much more.

Let us have courage, dear fellow people! Let us confront ourselves—it is worth it. For who would not like to gain the freedom that leads us out of confinement, out of our compulsions, the freedom that enables us to think great thoughts and ultimately, makes us happy from within!

Let us take a moment to think about ourselves. To think means to move. We bring into movement what corresponds to our thoughts, in order to look into the thoughts. Therefore, let us move the thoughts around the word freedom, and we will experience ourselves.

Let us take brief notes; we record in keywords what went on inside us.

So now we have experienced the content of our own thinking. It is as if a stranger is thinking, because those who very gradually analyze the content of their thinking and speaking initially think that what they are figuring out is not them.

Let us face the facts: What hurts us, what hits us, is not another—it is ourselves! If we recognize today what binds us, we have the chance to become free of it today.

Anyone who strives for a conscious life, who wants to become clear, sincere and free from within and find their way out of the narrow "ego-circle," the state of being caught in self-centeredness, will make an effort to grasp their sub-communications, what goes on underneath what they—consciously—think, speak or do.

These people get to know themselves more deeply than the superficial person. They gradually detach themselves from the binding to their own person, to their "personal," "human" and all-too-human aspects; they gain distance from themselves; they become better and better at mastering their own lives and are able to help and support others ever more selflessly, that is, without the desire for recognition and ovations of gratitude. They are increasingly impersonal, independent, self-reliant and free from within. Their horizon of consciousness expands; they attain a broad view, far-sightedness and an in-depth view, and in this way, become capable of truly bearing responsibility.

Binding means a loss of energy

Therefore, binding is unfreedom. A link makes us free. A true friendship is the link between those people who give to one another, but do not expect anything from each other. Let us become aware that the one who gives selflessly will also receive. True love, true friendship is positive communication, is giving and receiving, without expectation. That is the link; that is what we should strive for—that makes us free and happy.

A mutual attitude of expectation makes us dependent. Every dependence is binding, that is, unfreedom. We then expect the others to confirm us again and again, and the others expect this of us. This leads to compulsions.

Every confirmation from others leads to "cronyism," which usually does not last long.

Freedom also means, among other things, doing justice to our neighbor, with whom we may be together for years. Through this, independence and true freedom develop.

To be just to oneself, that is, honest with oneself, also brings justice and honesty toward our fellow people. This makes us free!

If we are just to ourselves, then we also weigh things in regard to others and do not bind them with words or gestures. If we are dishonest with ourselves, we bind ourselves to our neighbor. However, if we are honest with ourselves, we also leave our fellow people their freedom.

Let us be aware that our lack of freedom, which means our binding to people and to external security, is a loss of strength, because binding always takes energy from us. Those who bind themselves to us, by whom we allow ourselves to be bound, take energy from us. This means that over time our body also suffers from a lack of energy, causing many a weak organ to fall ill, so that we end up suffering under our lack of freedom.

It should become clear to us that every thought that involves a wanting, an expectation or even a claim, a demand on our neighbor, means a disturbance of unity. Every disturbance of unity first of all brings distraction in our thoughts, distress in our feelings, and, further along, indisposition and illness in the body. This is also true for being dogmatic and a know-it-all and having a reproachful attitude. We then find neither peace in ourselves nor peace with our fellow people.

Through our wanting, through binding thoughts, we attach ourselves to our neighbor. To wherever we think, we are trapped by it. If we don't want to let go, the one to whom we bind ourselves will ensnare us and rob us of more or less energy, thus enclosing us in his thought patterns, as it were. We are then caught therein—unfree, bound.

Binding, that is, unfreedom, also inevitably arises when we fail to live up to a responsibility. If, for example, we do not carry out tasks we have taken on, or do so only half-heartedly, negligently and inadequately, we become irresponsible over time.

People who do not keep their given word are unfree; they are unreliable; they lack steadfastness. Unfreedom leads to constantly leaning on others. People who are not trustworthy because they do not keep their word are always looking for like-minded people, that is, people who are as unfree as they are. They confirm each other. This leads to a so-called "mired life."

Once we have said "yes" and do not keep it, then we have broken our word. We may then become entangled in further promises, becoming our own prisoner over time.

How do we get out of this imprisonment when we may have bound ourselves to many, or even a great many, people to whom we promised something and did not keep it? These people are now the bars of our prison.

Thus, if we have promised something, we should keep it. However, before we make such a decision, we should question ourselves regarding our motives, and, before we give our "yes" to someone or say "yes" to something, we should examine it thoroughly: Is it according to God's will? Is it according to His commandments? Am I doing it voluntarily? Am I doing it out of conviction? Do I know that it corresponds to freedom? Then, after careful consideration and analysis, if we say "yes," we should keep it—otherwise we become our own prisoner. Since so many people mostly do not keep it, they have many, very many, problems and can hardly get out of their own prison.

Everyone is the architect of their good fortune or misfortune, because: Happiness or failure lie in the person himself.

Many people believe that freedom depends on property and possessions. Let us be aware that truly wealthy people are not those who think only of themselves, who hoard and accumulate possessions. Every excessive personal possession makes a person dependent on his possessions and demeans him. But those who use their wealth for new works, for pathways that others can follow, which then also lead to abundance for many, are truly free, because they have become rich within.

True love makes us free

Let us realize that true love makes us free. Only those who love God know that God loves them. This realization leads to absolute freedom.

But those who do not love God look for external support; they bind themselves to people and to the world. As a result, they also create doctrines and dogmas.

The word of the adversary of God is for binding. His principle is: "Divide, bind and rule." Binding does not link and leads to unfreedom. There is no system of rulership that was not based on binding and dependence.

In contrast, in the law of God, it is: "Link and be," which means selfless love, equality, freedom and unity—the brotherli-sisterliness with and for one another, the peaceableness that is practiced. The basic rules—equality, freedom, unity, brotherliness and from these, justice—are the basis for a peaceful togetherness among people. They are the ones who would turn members of a belligerent Christian western world into peaceable people.

True followers of Jesus, the Christ, are upright people who see clearly, who follow their living conscience, the inner ethical-moral control authority—alert, self-responsible, thinking and acting in an independent way.

Find your way to connect, to a true friendship

How can we find the connection that, for instance, characterizes true friendship? True friendship means to forgive one another again and again, to keep the commandments of God and to orient ourselves by the Sermon on the Mount of Jesus, the Christ. From this, develop freedom, true friendship and peace.

The divine in human beings is the alert heart of the soul; it is the faithfulness to the Eternal One; it is the clear view and the fulfillment of the will of God. Such people are far removed from the common motive force of those who speak of freedom but are unfree.

Those people in whom love and truth are one will not cavort in the anchorages of the world, not even when there are situations in which they think they are adrift on the high seas. Their God-consciousness is their strength. Whoever has attained this strength will neither judge nor condemn; they remain linked to love and truth in their striving and living. Reverence for the supreme law, which is love and neighborly love, is their obligation.

Every soul longs for freedom. We feel it in our feelings and in our conscience.

A sentence that we can move in us if we want to—a sentence not only for today:
Free is the one to whom the day belongs.

Those who do not become free always shatter everything that is good. Let us look at our world—this lack of freedom! Everyone wants only to be courted by the other. For this they start wars; through this they end up in dependence and much more. In the end, the aggrandizement before the other shows one's own weakness; that is unfreedom. Every war, also in thoughts, is against the neighbor—and is nothing but one's own weakness. When nations wage wars, whoever attacks is always the weaker.

War—whether in thought, whether in word, whether one country acts with armed force against another—war is always weakness.

Freedom is a gift from the Father. From freedom, can truly develop the inner love and the inner link to the soul of our fellow people, but also, above all, the communication with God, our Father. Then we no longer look at our fellow people, expecting them to do something for us—we are free within ourselves to develop the love for God.

If we free ourselves from what still binds us, through daily self-observation and clearing it up, then gradually freedom will develop that gives us the strength to help others selflessly here and there, without thinking of ourselves. For the purpose of our existence on Earth is to regain communication with freedom, with the divine in us, in order to sense what God has in mind for us in this world. We should not always be content to follow only our personal path from cradle to grave, but God wants that we, after a certain time, have acquired the inner maturity, that is, the inner freedom, so that we can sense our neighbor, in order to serve and to help our neighbor.

If we strive to follow the instructions of the Sermon on the Mount in the situations of our everyday life, for example, by giving up any fight against our neighbor, by recognizing in ever finer nuances the belligerence in our feelings, sensations and thoughts and defeating it with the help and through the power of the Inner Christ, then His light will shine in us more and more, and we will experience His workings in everyday life in manifold ways.

Those who learn to experience and sense Christ in themselves gain inner support, independence, inner security and strength—gifts of the Most High that are indestructible because God's power, love and wisdom are everlasting.

So let us become free, to be free! To be free is a quality of life; to be free is peace; to be free is love and unity.

> Therefore: Become free, and be free!

Prologues and Monologues

*From a teaching hour with Gabriele
for the Free Communities Under the Sign of the Lily
in October 2017*

his topic is of above average importance: It is about the prologues and monologues.

Many ask themselves, "What can that be—prologues, monologues?"

When we hear about our "thoughts," that's quite normal for us, because everyone has thoughts, they are a part of our life. Many thoughts are ultimately there to be questioned or analyzed, so that what is not good can be recognized and remedied in time.

We should recognize our not-good thoughts in time and remedy them in good time before they become prologues or even turn into monologues.

Thus we come to our topic: prologues, monologues.

A prologue is composed of similar thoughts; it can be termed the thought-base or the basis for monologues.

A thought-base is a first sign for a prologue, which, depending on its progression and circumstances can be a prelude to a monologue, perhaps with dramatic consequences, depending on the content of the thoughts.

The longer we nurture one or more thoughts of the same kind, the more they form themselves into a so-called nest of conjoined thoughts.

The monologues start from a so-called "nest," from a thought-base, when we do not recognize in time the nest, the prologue of like thoughts, and rectify it. The prelude to monologues is, therefore, the so-called nest or a still convoluted chain of like thoughts. The chain of thoughts, which has gradually unwound, forms the monologues.

Let us return to the prologue, to the nest of like thoughts or a convoluted chain of thoughts.

Usually, a prologue begins with a situation that has not been dealt with, which leads us repeatedly to the same or similar thoughts.

We think and think about what we could not deal with, also about problems, worries and fears, as well as about inconsistencies at work, perhaps with the boss, but also in the partnership, etc., etc.

For each person there is something different behind it. The forerun to a prologue, which may have a dramatic aftermath, is therefore fundamentally different.

If we do not resolve the prologue in time, then it becomes a monologue that can continue for days.

Prologues and monologues are conversations with ourselves. We talk to ourselves, and, at that, always about the same thing. We think and think the same kind of thoughts over and over again. It is the then unwinding chain of thoughts that started from the prologue and continued in the monologues. Thus, we talk to ourselves; we think the same thing over and over again.

This chain of thoughts can, as stated, continue for days. A prologue, a so-called nest of thoughts, may include further thoughts that are derived from the same or similar situations, possibly from conversations with people who have experienced the same or similar things.

A part of these thought-conversations is then included in the personal prologue or in the monologue, so that a further sequence of images possibly results—because people think in images. Depending on the image sequences, that is, pictorial situations, these can be added to the prologue or the monologue.

Wrong thoughts, no matter of what kind, can be attracted by people; these are thoughts that can, in turn, come from people or even from other forces. Monologues, depending on their content, can thus drive people to dramatic actions and lead to serious consequences.

That is why this topic: "Prologues and Monologues" is of above-average importance.

In our world, which is pervaded by war against human beings and the nature kingdoms, much can be derived from so-called prologues and monologues.

Nearly every day, we hear or read of riots, of looting, of thefts, of assaults or even of rapes, of manslaughter and murder.

One wonders: Where do such excesses come from?

What preceded all this?

At the end of the schooling hour, Gabriele suggested sharing about this topic and about one's own experiences, with the words:

We are called upon. Let us not talk about others—let us talk about ourselves. Our own experiences, not theory, can help our neighbor.

The Law of Correspondence

From a teaching hour with Gabriele
on April 15, 1988

What is the law of correspondence and where does it come from? Is it a part of our spiritual heritage?

Let us think of the highest radiant being—it is God, our eternal Father. God, our Father, is absolute love.

Is it possible that the highest radiant being, God, our Father, has correspondences?—No! So we have to ask ourselves: Then where do correspondences come from?

We are in the image of our Father. Our eternal Father has no correspondences; He is absolute, eternally flowing love. Our heritage is divine love. In divine love are peace, harmony, humility, kindness, Order, Will, Wisdom, Earnestness, Patience, Love and Mercy. That is our spiritual heritage. That is the macrocosm, the seven basic powers of God, and we have these seven basic powers in us. Thus, our inner being is the microcosm. In it are meekness, humility, kindness, the many, many powers that are contained in these seven basic powers.

Therefore, we could say that the law of correspondence was ultimately created by the Fall-beings, and all those who immerse in the Fall, that is, who burden themselves, build on the law of correspondence. Every burden, also called sin, is a low vibration in our soul, and the soul immediately responds to the same or similar things when they vibrate toward us. Therefore, we could then conclude that we have the same or similar thing in us when something vibrates toward us and we are irritated by it.

And how do we overcome this law of correspondence, how do we remedy what vibrates toward us, what irritates us? If we want to become perfect again, the conscious images of our eternal Father, radiant, pure spirit beings, then we must recognize many things that we have caused by means of our correspondences, because if there are large parts of correspondences that we do not experience, that we do not look at, we will reinforce them again and again. Therefore, self-recognition is a very essential factor for us, the basis, so that the Redeemer-light in us can grow stronger.

Christ brought us the Redeemer-spark, but redemption in each of us is not concluded until we no longer have correspondences. As long as we have correspondences, we are under the sign of redemption. Only once we have recognized and surrendered the correspondences and live the law of God more and more do we, as beings, come into the three filiation attributes, into the planes of preparation where we learn to work with the eternal law, that is, to control our spiritual body completely, every cosmic radiation, every spiritual atom.

To live in the law of correspondence is very dangerous. Because if we are not vigilant and do not immediately look at our agitations or surrender them to Christ, then we will continue to build on these correspondences, that is, burdens, also called sins. Yet each day, we are given the opportunity to experience the amount we should recognize on that day. This goes from early in the morning until late in the evening.

Many things that come toward us do not upset us. However, many things come toward us that cause us to feel a tingling inside; we feel resentment; we feel the rise of aggressiveness, of envy and much more. We see our neighbor, we like some things about him that we don't have—envy follows, we are envious. If we do not pay attention to it, this impulse passes us by. However, it is not gone, but merely postponed. Under certain circumstances—if we brood about the envy, about what our neighbor has that we don't have, and perhaps speak negatively about him—we will increase this complex of "envy," and at some point, it will come upon us more strongly.

Therefore, the days are a gift from God. And every morning when we wake up, we can be sure that God has placed us in this day because He has much to say to us on this day, today. If we live this day consciously, then we experience our correspondences; we experience memories and in the memories feel what we have already discarded. The correspondences cause a surge of emotion in us—the memories let us confidently realize with what effort and trouble we have discarded what vibrates toward us.

From this, also comes understanding for our fellow people, who are now still wrestling with the complex that we have overcome with much effort. From this develops the spiritual self-assurance and the inner attitude to help our neighbor as much as we can—in prayer, with encouraging words, or with the right impulses to carefully draw his attention to how we approached this problem to overcome it.

Each day we are given only as much as we are able to bear—unless we keep putting off something we should look at, merely thinking about it and thus increasing our correspondence, our burden or sin. Then the time may come when this massive complex breaks in over us, and at that moment we don't know how to begin to clear it all up. But if, at that moment, when we realize that several correspondences or a whole complex are coming at us, we pray and ask, "Lord, give me the chance to see how I can begin to break it down," then the help usually comes from within. We suddenly get clear—a part of the complex of correspondences comes to us, that is, feelings or thoughts of this complex intensify in us, and we realize, "Aha, that's where I now have to begin to clear this up."

However, when it comes to smaller correspondences, often just brief negative thoughts, we can surrender them to Christ and confront them as soon as they come back and say, "No, I'm not thinking like that anymore; I now consciously think positively." Then Christ transforms this negative force into positive energy. This then causes the Redeemer-light to grow stronger in us.

Once we have worked through our larger correspondences with Christ and surrendered them to Him, then these correspondences become memories. If the same or similar things vibrate toward us again, then we experience within that we remain calm and self-possessed, and at the same time, the impulse comes: "Yes, I have overcome that." And we also sense in our inner being how we overcame it: Aspects then come up on how we tackled the whole thing, the whole correspondence, and thus cleared it up with Christ. Through this, we can, in turn, help our neighbor who is in a same or similar situation.

We come to another topic:

How do I become peaceful?

We often want to achieve inner peace very quickly, because ultimately, discord disturbs us. Our soul longs for peace, for security—but our person often does the opposite. Why?

Could the basis for more quickly achieving peace within us be the trust in God? Let us think about it: In many cases, why do we attack our neighbor, why do we quarrel with him? We say it is our correspondences. Yes, it may very well be our correspondences, but if we trust in God, we will be able to speak with our neighbor calmly and clearly. So the basis for coming to peace more quickly is the trust in God.

However, if we have little or no trust in God, then fear comes more and more, and from fear, aggression, and from aggression, fighting—and ultimately, war.

When we trust in God, we can say in a different way what moves us. Let us think about the word "moves" for a moment. We move something; ultimately, it is the correspondence. If we go to God with this correspondence and say, "Lord, it is a correspondence, but as it comes up in me now, I don't want to say it to my neighbor; I trust in Your guidance," then, at that moment, a kind of gentleness comes into our inner being, and we suddenly feel how we can express what we are feeling with other words, and our neighbor is understanding and may even respond to our words. A positive communication takes place, and many a thing can thus also be cleared up very well.

Jesus, the Christ, said, *"Become like the little children."* Let us look at this thought: Become like the little children. Then, as soon as we become like the little children, our eternal Father is also closer to us. If we switch off our intellect somewhat more and see ourselves not only as a human being, but also as the child of God who loves the Father above all, then we can also meet our Father in a more childlike way.

Let us assume the following: Some thought or other comes toward us, or something is said to us—at that moment, the correspondence rises up, anger or aggression or envy or whatever it is. If we then very briefly say or call to within, "Father, not like this!" which means, "Not like it is now coming up in me!"—at that same moment, strength comes, and we feel that we can more easily overcome this correspondence or approach our neighbor with completely different words.

The help is there—through this we also sense how God, the Spirit of our eternal Father, is close to us. This sensing gives confidence to place before Him again and again everything that troubles us, or to call out at every upsurge of a correspondence: "Father, not like this!"

From trust comes peace, and peace, in turn, bears within the self-assurance to stand above the human aspects and to look more closely at ourselves and clear up more quickly what is still human in us. Let us allow the Father to work in us, and let us endeavor to be more like children, not childish, but the child; the call "Father"—and the Spirit of our Father is active in us.

The Disease-causing Subconscious and Life

*From a seminar with Gabriele
in 2002*

Many of us know that we think and speak in images and that these images have content. Yet we rarely experience our behavior patterns pictorially. Why is that so?

For one thing, our thought processes run much too fast, and for another, we usually speak too quickly and without control. Therefore, it is also not possible for us to question our thoughts and conversations to grasp what they may trigger. Because of this, we usually do not know what we are storing. Many of us also know the terms "conscious mind," "subconscious" and "superconscious," or "spirit-consciousness." But these words often mean little to us—simply because we are satisfied with idioms, terms and clichés without figuring out their meaning and significance for us.

Let us bring to mind that thoughts and words, or terms, are forms, as it were, capsules, shells. In these lies the essence, their content, which expresses itself in images. So behind all our thoughts and words run images, sequences of images, which we store pictorially in the conscious mind and subconscious as well as in our soul, and beyond that, in corresponding planetary constellations.

Most people are not aware that they store, nor of what they store. Our brain, the conscious mind and subconscious, is a storage medium that stores pictorially according to the content of our thoughts and words, from which results our entire behavior.

We have to distinguish between inputs in the conscious mind and inputs in the subconscious. The images in the conscious mind are shaped by our illusory world. The imagery of our conscious mind includes what we think we represent and are, that is, what we pretend to ourselves. These images deceive us.

On the other hand, the subconscious does not take in our illusory images, for example, how good and noble we are. It pictorially stores exactly—

without any influence—the real content of our thoughts, words and actions, what we want to hide from others and from ourselves, our ignoble impulses, feelings, claims and ambitions. It is the subliminal that does not like to be seen, that is, to be clearly recognized, because that would expose us. The subconscious is incorruptible. It does not deceive itself even when it reflects to us our all-too-human aspects or memories from our past.

Consequently, the conscious mind and subconscious are usually at odds. The conscious mind stores our imaginary, or illusory, world, that is, what we think we are. The subconscious does not argue or use tactics; it does not weigh—it reacts; in the rhythm of the days it sends what it has stored, and it does so in images.

Our conscience is the scale of feelings between the subconscious, the soul, and the superconscious, the spirit-consciousness. The superconscious, the spirit-consciousness in us, is the eternally pure; it is the core of being; it is the Spirit of God in us, which places the laws of the universe on the scale, on our emotional scale. If we have not learned to question and analyze what our conscious mind often deludes us into thinking, then we suppress our conscience; it becomes lazy and dull.

Let us be aware that if God, the spirit-consciousness in the human being, (also called the superconscious) cannot place any admonishing and helping impulses on the scale of our conscience, the same as the scale of our feelings, because we do not question and analyze our thoughts, words and patterns of behavior—that is, because we do not figure out what we have entered into the subconscious so as to correct it in time—then we block the scale of our feelings, the scale of our conscience, and work exclusively with our conscious mind. This, however, constantly gives us misinformation, thoughts, words and behavior patterns, which we are convinced are correct. We believe: This is true—nevertheless, it is merely an illusory reality that we have created ourselves, and that includes all the knowledge that we have learned and read about.

Just with our phrases such as "I assume that it is so" or "I mean" or "In my opinion," etc., we can recognize that we lack self-recognition and analytical thinking. With these phrases, which are idioms with a content that corresponds to us, we state that we have not understood ourselves, that we say or think something of which we ourselves have "no idea."

Those who live in this self-deception often think they are clever and wise. They have not given their conscience any training. They do not want to look at themselves, to analyze themselves. Such people waste their existence. They are satisfied with the self-congratulation they have given to their conscious mind, with which they are in constant correspondence, until one day the subconscious mind is full and then expresses itself as fate.

All cells, all cellular tissues, the organs and all other components of our body have a so-called compound consciousness, which likewise consists of conscious mind, subconscious and superconscious, that is, spirit-consciousness. Our mindscape, all that we uncontrolledly express, is stored by the conscious mind in those components of our body that vibrationally fit with our complex, superficial thinking, talking and acting. The storing takes place according to the principle of like attracts like. The subconscious, on the other hand, stores the content of our patterns of thinking and behaving in the corresponding components of our body. Thus, we realize that our organism and all the functions of our body are in constant communication with our brain, the conscious mind and subconscious, and that storing is constantly taking place, being imprinted in our body through our feeling, sensing, thinking, speaking and acting.

And what about the spirit-consciousness in every cell of our body? This is an absolute authority that cannot be influenced. The spirit-consciousness is the original source, the Being, God, the absolute law. Therefore, the spirit-consciousness cannot be deceived by the conscious mind or the subconscious. It is absolute and perfect; it is the helper, the admonisher, the guide in us.

If we have not learned to listen to the superconscious, the spirit-consciousness, if we have not let the scales, the feeling, the conscience, weigh and speak, if we have not questioned ourselves, and if we have not repented, cleared up and dissolved with the help of our inner Guide and Helper what is in us that is against the Divine, then gradually the subconscious fills up and becomes autonomous.

An autonomous subconscious has largely switched off the scales of feeling and conscience. It merely acts. This means that the conscious mind can hardly give orders to the subconscious anymore. The subconscious has taken on a life of its own.

The autonomous subconscious has no thoughts, it has no conscience—it executes. According to our negative energetic inputs, it acts on our body, on those organs and components with which it is most intensely in correspondence.

Negative energies have the corresponding negative effects. Thus, a person's negative inputs, such as envy, arrogance, wanting to be and to have, but also self-pity, resignation, fatalism and fears, transform down the vibration of certain organs in his body, which are thus weakened and their function disturbed. Consequently, these organs can then no longer fulfill their tasks as intended, which can lead to illnesses.

The effects of the negative energies that we created through our negative behavior in previous incarnations and in this incarnation can also affect other areas of our life on Earth, depending on what inputs are active. Worries, blows of fate, suffering, misfortunes of all kinds can appear. There may also be triggers of various kinds in the individual—we are always the ones who cause them.

Instead of now questioning the initial symptoms, the first disturbances that our body, for example, transmits to us, regretting the recognized wrong attitudes, clearing them up with the help of the inner Helper and Advisor and not doing them anymore, or instead of affirming the positive in the symptoms, thereby mobilizing the self-healing forces, we affirm the disturbances and the beginning illness in our body.

We also often brood over worries and problems in our thoughts until they become a breeding ground for disease. With our brooding thoughts we attract the corresponding germs. If the person decreases his body vibration by revolving around himself, then the brain is also able to perform less and less. Conditions of weakness of various kinds set in. In old age, the body becomes more immobile; the legs don't really want to move anymore. The brain's lethargy becomes noticeable in the whole body.

We continue to affirm these symptoms, which are the faulty circuits of our thinking and acting, and which the autonomous subconscious transfers to our body, because we continue to complain about our ailments and complain that no one helps us, not even the physician. How can the physician help us? Can he make us well if we constantly reinforce and amplify what is flowing out of our autonomous subconscious by moaning and complaining and thus putting our whole body into a vibration that causes further ailments, difficulties and diseases?

Our life on Earth is precious! Day after day, God, the Eternal, gives each of us His high energy so that we can recognize and overcome burdens, negative energies that we created in previous incarnations and in this life on Earth, in order to grow more and more into a life in His Spirit.

But if we use the spiritual strength given to us to let it flow into negative, self-centeredness, this is a misuse of this divine gift that does not lead us to salvation.

Thus, we are also often too negligent with ourselves and with the gift of our earthly life, by affirming illness, suffering, problems, fate and the like, over and over again. We revolve around our ego, wasting much divine energy and reducing our brain activity. It is not surprising that we then complain of headaches and forgetfulness or nervousness and insecurity.

Apart from a memory loss possibly caused by brain damage, each of us has brain activity, a memory capacity of unimaginable performance. Of course, the brain must be trained to be positive.

We often hear, "I'm forgetful." Or, "I can't remember numbers." Or, "I can't remember what you are saying, I have to write it down." Or, "I'm too tired to think about it." Forgetfulness sets in through indifference. Without thought or interest, we take in what others tell us.

If we get to the bottom of the indifference, we inevitably encounter our self-centeredness. We have our own apparent well-being, our interests, our benefit in mind—how our fellow people feel is all the same to us. This is the lethargy and coldness of the heart that afflicts humankind.

Every negativity is a negative autosuggestion, an imprint on our subconscious. With it we block processes in our body. The lethargy of our mind causes us to affirm the negativity or to misuse others for our own purposes. This already happens when we say, for example, "Remind me, please, because I forget so easily," or when we say, "I must write that down so I don't forget," or "Yes, you said similar things to me; I forgot." These are negative affirmations, which make the activity of our memory slacken, that is, they reduce the brain activity. With this, we ultimately command the subconscious to weaken our body, to reduce the efficiency of the organs.

Let us not forget that what is active in the subconscious is also in movement in our soul and in the repository of the corresponding planetary constellation. If we affirm our indisposition and our illness, then we store unceasingly in the conscious mind. These are further wrong attitudes, or faulty circuits. We store the strengthening of the indisposition, we store the content of the illness, the weakness and much more.

Due to the split between our world of thoughts and our way of speaking, a faulty circuit occurs in our brain; the abused positive forces lead to tiredness, weakness and a poor performance; the resulting despondency leads to failure, forgetfulness, omission and much more. We should learn to question our split ways of thinking and speaking, to repair the faulty circuits in our brain, that is, to dissolve them step by step with the Spirit of life and to supply our brain with the positive forces that we affirm over and over again, that is, to consciously and systematically specify them until the new, positive program takes effect in the brain and in the body.

Let it be repeated: The pictorial material that we store in the subconscious through our daily negative feeling, sensing, thinking, speaking and acting, we also store in our soul and in the corresponding planetary constellation of the material and immaterial cosmos of the purification planes. These stored inputs bring about in the material cosmos a matrix picture, the new human being for a future incarnation. In this incarnation of ours, the subconscious reflects a part of our matrix image; therefore, it is the mirror image of our body in one of our next incarnations.

Let us bring to mind once again: In the conscious mind are our willful inputs, ideas and points of view that are fallacious; they are programs of deception. We believe that we are what we think, say and do.

In contrast, the subconscious stores the content of what we express from ourselves. It may make us correspondingly ill.

The superconscious, the spirit-consciousness, is the life; it is our true, eternal reality.

Let us again become aware of the following, in order to imprint it on us: Starting from the brain, all instructions are transmitted via the nervous system to muscles, organs, to every cell, to every blood vessel, to all the building blocks of our body. All functions of our body are determined by the conscious mind and subconscious. So every function, every single cell of our body is in correspondence with the conscious mind and subconscious.

As already stated, every cell of our body also has a superconscious, a spirit-consciousness. If the Spirit of God cannot reach us because we do not turn to Him, that is, if we do not dissolve the blockages, the negative aspects in the subconscious and in our soul, then we experience our blows of fate, even up to the most serious illness.

Often we say, "I affirm the health in me." This affirmation is right and good. But we must ask ourselves: What have we been entering into our subconscious for years, decades? Does it accept our affirmation, or does it autonomously send the negative?

Training the brain could stimulate the reversal of our conscious mind and subconscious, so that the disease-causing subconscious receives the appropriate positive signals from the conscious mind and gradually adjusts to them.

The prerequisite for something being able to change in us is the realization of what needs to change. So it is necessary to question our thinking, talking and acting in order to gradually find out who we really are and what is stored in our subconscious, which may have a massive effect on our body.

Training the brain is decisively determined by the direction of our thoughts. As long as our thinking is negative, we direct our brain impulses in the wrong direction. We not only waste energy, but also make ourselves sick.

If we want to train our brain to be positive, then we must take time to do so. For example, if we affirm the health of our body, the health of certain organs, then we should pause at each affirmation and wait for the reaction of our body.

If we practice this first step, then very soon we will notice a movement in our solar plexus, a kind of "grumbling." Our nervous system is signaling, for example, that the subconscious is sending other impulses. If we take the time to perceive these nerve impulses in the conscious mind, we may experience images from the subconscious, contents of our behavior patterns that we were not aware of before, but which are decisive, for example, for heart problems, stomach ailments and the like. We should let these images have an effect on us, so that we can take a closer look at them. The images have an effect on our disposition. Very gradually, what is bothering our body will crystallize.

If with the help of the Inner Helper and Adviser, we repent, clear up the wrong attitudes, the faulty circuits in the body, and no longer think and do the same and similar things, then we develop a sensitivity that turns inward. As a result, the scales of feelings and conscience are restored. Then the Spirit of God is able to place His help, His healing, but also His admonishing impulses onto this scale, because we allow Him to do so and are willing to accept and use His power.

Through a conscious affirmation, which is accompanied by clearing up the then emerging all-too-human aspects, we experience a greater dynamism of our brain activity, which leads to an increase of physical energy.

Those who look deeper and question themselves are not deceived by their subconscious. So this means to train the brain, to explore the subconscious, to let the images come, to look at them, in order to clear up what harms us with the help of the Spirit of God.

I repeat: Through a healthy spiritual training of the brain, we activate the self-healing powers, so that we can gain increased performance, well-being and health. Let us not forget: Spiritually active people enjoy good general health.

We should make ourselves aware each day anew: Every thought presses for realization in our environment and also in our body.

But let us also be aware that with every truly positive thought, with every holistic, lawful word and with every action willed by God, we not only strengthen our memory, but also activate our conscious mind and subconscious in a positive sense and strengthen our body. This also means that the force field, our aura, becomes lighter and brighter, and thus, a magnet for more positive forces.

Our existence on Earth—which, according to our human viewpoint, consists of days—is the best teacher. Human beings can be capable of learning from birth to death, provided they are willing to learn.

Learning also means a change of thinking, a consistent practicing and training, in order to repeatedly point the wrong way of thinking in the right direction, and thus achieve a reprogramming to the positive through the power of life.

We have to learn to affirm the good, but also to look at the negative, to rectify it with the help of the divine consciousness in us and not do it anymore. Once we have recognized some of the negative aspects and repented and cleared them up with the eternal Spirit, we will input the positive in our conscious mind. If we stay with the affirmation of what God wants, then in time our subconscious will react and transmit the positive aspects coming from us to the body.

A great help for an alert, concentrated and conscientious way of life would be to adopt a correspondingly upright inner and outer posture already in the morning and to maintain this throughout the day as much as possible. If the processes of our thinking, speaking and acting are carried out in a disciplined manner, if we strive to go through the changing daily situations in a collected, conscious and straightforward manner, we save a lot of energy and remain calm, level-headed and fresh until late in the evening.

We could prescribe for ourselves, for example:

What you think, think completely.

What you say, say consciously.

What you do, be totally concentrated. Be completely with everything, with your thoughts, words and actions.

We should learn not to be distracted by anything or anyone. Only in this way can we learn intense concentration. Those who stay collected also stay mentally awake. They open their conscious mind and subconscious for the superconscious, the Spirit. No external suggestion can affect them.

In this way, we reverse the subconscious to the positive, so that the positive, the healing, the helping forces in our body become active and we learn to understand the language of the organs. While we learn to activate our brain in a positive sense, to strengthen our memory, we experience mental alertness and above all, concentration. This results in a wide range of receptivity, which we experience in vivid images.

Let us take up the following once again:

Conscious, positive training of our brain increases retentiveness and also improves memory. A mentally efficient brain develops creative thinking and alertness, to receive the superconscious, the spirit-consciousness.

We can put ourselves to the test. Let us ask ourselves: How is it with our ability to retain and remember? Can we remember people and when they said something and what they said? Can we remember individual experiences with fellow people? What were our reactions and behavior? There are many ways to check what and how much our memory has stored.

If we train our brain to be positive, we gain inner peace. We will give rest to our body at the right time. We will listen to the language of our body and eat healthy food. We will gradually do our work with the superconscious, the Spirit in us, and concentrate on everything we do.

A positively active brain, a healthy, conscious memory is a great treasure, a helper in our work, in the family, in everything we think, say and do.

We become capable of noticing things, energetic and joyfully active, receptive and open to the great things in life. We feel the well-being of our body. We notice the healthy currents, which are also healing currents. We are strong in learning and highly efficient, a conscious thinker and speaker, who acts in accordance with the Spirit.

Following are some examples of questions from seminar participants and answers given by Gabriele, which may also be helpful for the reader:

Question: The conscious mind serves, after all, to take in my "semblance," and the subconscious, the negative. I actually assumed that. But the subconscious also takes in the positive, if I now contrast this ...

Gabriele: The subconscious absorbs the positive for a while until the negative is transformed into the positive in the soul and in the constellation of the stars. Then the negative is deleted in the subconscious.

What is of importance for our future remains as memory in the subconscious, but not as guilt. The negative that is transformed into the positive in the subconscious through our remorse and clearing it up—with the help of the Christ of God—must also gradually transform in the physical body. The positive in the body also has a helping and healing effect. It is the power of Christ.

This process of transformation, of support, clears the way to the spirit-consciousness, to the Spirit of God, which is then able to guide us more and more.

Question: When I get into a situation, the subconscious controls me, sometimes more, sometimes less. That is how I experience it. It then tells me what negativity I have input.

Gabriele: Here we have to be alert and differentiate: Is it the conscious mind that confirms our momentary thoughts? Or is it the subconscious that says something entirely different?

So there are two components. The conscious mind confirms our way of thinking; it is the capsules, the shells of our thoughts, that which we believe we are. The subconscious, on the other hand, sends other signals. It transmits to us who we really are, what is cavorting in our thoughts and ideas. In such situations, we realize that we are divided into two parts. If we are alert, we quickly realize that the subconscious is stronger than the conscious mind.

We have to learn to figure ourselves out, for example, what we think in the conscious mind and what corresponds to the content of our thoughts and words. Let's remember: The content of our thoughts and words, of our whole behavior, is stored in the subconscious. Everything else is just shells of words or thoughts that the conscious mind stores.

The New Person—How Do I Stay True to My Resolutions?

From a teaching hour with Gabriele on January 7, 1996

To make a resolution means we intend to do something; we commit ourselves to something. Thus, if we intend to do something, then we have not yet fulfilled it. Therefore, decisive is: What do we want to now do differently? And how did we do it in past years?

The one says: "I want to stop smoking." Another says: "I want to practice discipline" or "I want to grow closer to God."

We always hear "I want to." But this does not yet mean "I am disciplined," I have stopped smoking," "I am in God" or "I am closer to God." Thus, the "I want to" tells us that we are not yet the way we have resolved to be. So, the goal is a resolution.

And we must strive for this resolution day after day. It must remain in our awareness. It must anchor, as it were, in the conscious mind and in the subconscious. We cannot do this by saying today, "I want to become more disciplined" or "I want to grow closer to God." This "I want to" must be before our eyes at every moment, then, when we fall back into our old habits. It must be revived in the conscious mind and the subconscious. Only once it has come to life in the conscious mind and the subconscious, do we have the strength to remedy what lies behind the resolution, namely, the negligence, the lack of discipline, the indifference, the distance from God, and much, much more.

When we make a resolution, then what we have done up to now will not disappear. It should and must be worked on, because we don't want to keep doing the same thing anymore. In order to stop doing it, we have to make an effort and declare war on the "old Adam." It is a struggle, but the struggle is worth it, namely, when we take into our conscious mind and our subconscious, the positive, that is, the positive thoughts, the positive inputs as a reminder. The link with Christ then gives us the strength to work on what still remains, what lies in the "want to." So that means that what we want to remedy is still in the conscious mind and the subconscious and ultimately, in our soul and beyond that, in the stars and planets, for they are the inputs, and these are based on our way of feeling, sensing, thinking, speaking and acting.

We want to do things differently; we have chosen a good resolution—and this resolution must first come alive. So every day, first of all in the evening before going to bed, we ought to commit ourselves to this good, Christian resolution—I deliberately say "Christian resolution," which is based on the commandments, on the laws of God. When we resolve for this resolution, first of all in the evening, then the subconscious first absorbs it, and then gradually, the soul. When we are deeply asleep, the soul goes its way into the worlds beyond, according to our state of consciousness, but it has this resolution with it and in the worlds of the beyond, it will come to grips with this resolution. For the soul may meet like-minded beings; it comes into a sphere of vibration in which it hears about these things, about how it can realize the Christian resolution in the earthly garment. With these experiences from the worlds beyond, it then comes back as our sleep grows lighter; and when we awaken, it is again fully in the body.

We have entered the resolution into the conscious mind and subconscious. It is there as a magnet and pulls into the subconscious and then into the conscious mind what the soul worked out on its pathways while we were fast asleep. Suddenly positive thoughts come. In the morning we suddenly feel that there is something in us that gives us new strength, new courage. In the morning, we ask Christ that on this day we can keep this resolution, that we can practice it, that we can put it into practice. So already in the morning, in our prayer, we take up this Christian resolution. It is then not just a thought that we chose some time or other, like, for instance, "I want to grow closer to God," but this resolution then gradually builds up: How do I grow closer to God? What am I going to do today?

Suddenly, problems come up during the day. Our resolution, which is growing more and more, which comes more and more alive in our conscious mind and subconscious, admonishes us and leads us to a conversation, possibly to a lawful solution.

Should we have forgotten our resolution by lunchtime—we do this when it has not yet come alive in our conscious mind and subconscious—then we should briefly withdraw and enter this resolution—I emphasize, this Christian resolution, that is, according to the commandment of the love for God and neighbor—in ourselves again, and make ourselves aware that: "I now enter this resolution of mine into my conscious mind, into my subconscious, and also into my soul and I give it to my soul to take along."

This instantly leads to a momentary communication with the Spirit of the Christ of God in us. And we will then not only repeat our resolution, but we will also direct several heartfelt prayer-thoughts to Christ. If it is only five to seven minutes at noontime, that's enough; even if it is only three minutes—that's enough. If these three minutes are heartfelt, then we will have done more for our soul and for our body than when we sit for 10 minutes for a superficial meditation and simply repeat in our conscious mind what we have resolved for. We then again have the strength for the afternoon, our resolution takes hold. Christ comes alive in our resolution and is the Admonisher. He is also the One who reminds us, who admonishes us again and again when we fall back into our our old habits, and at the same time gives us impulses about how, for example, we should behave at work, how we can start and finish a job. He gives us strength for our work. He encourages us in conversations and much more.

Then in the evening, just before going to bed, we again enter our resolution into our conscious mind and subconscious and again give it to the soul to take along on its journey. If we do this earnestly, indeed, if we earnestly want to become new people in the Spirit of the Christ of God, then we will be stronger each morning. Our soul will become more light-filled, and we will gain much more strength. Our resolution or resolutions then are more alive in us. They are the admonishers, the guides, the controllers. Our prayers will grow deeper, our thoughts more positive, our life more conscious. We will then also have the strength to clear up all the sinfulness that the day points out to us, because the good, indeed, the truly Christian, resolutions are alive in us. They are aspects of the Christ of God in us that admonish us, that remind us, that guide and direct us.

After all, resolutions are inputs, and inputs are seismographs—they seek exactly what still lies behind the resolution, what could disturb or has disturbed the resolution. If, with Christ, we clear up what we have recognized, then we draw closer to the actualization of our resolution.

For example, a resolution might be: We need to be more responsible for ourselves. To be responsible for ourselves means we are also responsible before God for what we think, speak and do. The moment we realize: "I am responsible to God for everything I think, say and do," we will also change our lives in a positive sense. But this then also means responsibility toward our neighbor.

To please God is a high aspiration, and yet to achieve our divine heritage is a lofty goal. If we remind ourselves of this again and again, in every situation, even when things get hard: "I want to please God," then the inner light will give us the answer again and again: "Stop; please God!" That is then the answer from our resolution: "Stop; please God!" And then we also know what to do.

Thus, the new person. How do I remain true to my resolutions? How?
Keep it up, Christ upholds you!

The Language of the Soul via Feelings and Moods

From a seminar of the same title with Gabriele in 2007

The love for God and neighbor is the deepest engraving in our soul, because it is the center of our spiritual body, the heart of our true being.

The love for God and neighbor harasses neither human being nor animal.

Heavenly love expects nothing. It is the word that finds expression only in the depth of the inner heart.

The love for God and neighbor does not bind.
It does not judge and condemn.
It is impersonal.

Most people are constantly in an attitude of expectation. Wherever they look, feelings and thoughts come up in them that contain expectations toward their fellow people. Even when we evaluate one of our neighbors, the expectation is always central; for example, we want to "prove" to ourselves and our surroundings that we are better than the other person. Whether man or woman—we want to be more beautiful, more attractive, more appealing and more intelligent than the other.

An attitude of expectation always corresponds to self-love. We want something for ourselves and, ultimately, at the expense of the energy of our fellow people.

Our expectations are mostly rooted in our feelings, which can gradually develop into passion and all-too-human love, depending on what we have entered into our conscious mind and subconscious. And many a person experiences that passion always creates new suffering, which is, after all, always the old.

Those who have learned to immerse in the very basis of their true being, in the love for God and neighbor, do not expect anything. Nor do they have a passionate character, regardless of what kind.

True love makes no claims because it possesses what many people pursue day after day: inner happiness, contentment, security and other priceless values.

True love finds comfort in God and receives inner well-being from God.

People in the love for God and neighbor feel solely as "embodied ones"—they consciously live in their human bodies as beings in God. They act and work through their "vehicle," the physical body. Those who have raised their consciousness to the infinite, to the divine, do not ask who they are—they know it; they are aware of it.

People in the love for God and neighbor feel their spiritual heart pulsating. They do not waste energy, because love gives, because love comforts, because love helps.

To the one who lives as an infinite being in his body, the reactions of his neighbor show the extent to which he is allowed to approach his neighbor, his fellow people, be it in helping them, in giving comfort and so on.

People in the love for God and neighbor are always willing to give and to help, to the extent that their neighbor wants this.

Whoever has learned to live in the physical body as a spiritual being is in God's omnipotence and feels the stream of cosmic power, the love and wisdom. To live as a spiritual eternal being in the earthly garment means to be sensitive to the power of the Spirit and permeable for the Divine, the eternal stream.

Only through order and constant self-monitoring—which could be called "discipline"—and through practice will human beings learn and experience that their true being is not of this world.

What is the meaning of "discipline"?
Discipline means: self-discipline; overcoming our human indolence and negligence, also with regard to our all-too-human thoughts and sinful inclinations. Through self-discipline, through practice and through spiritual learning, by turning inward, we become permeable to the power of the

light and become the being who consciously lives in the physical body.

Some will now object, "But isn't it very difficult to maintain order and discipline?"

However, I can say: It is indeed possible! For Jesus said to us people: *You shall be perfect, as your Father in heaven is perfect.*

And if that were not possible, then Jesus, the Christ, would not have taught it to us!

Without the commitment to order and self-discipline—which results in spiritual learning and thus, inner, spiritual growth—negative thoughts, spiteful words, envy, resentment, strife and the like have power over us, because we keep nourishing them with the same things.

In order to find the love for God and neighbor, to find our true being, so that we can experience and come to know that in our body there is a being from God's omnipotence and love, we must above all overcome our all-too-human, partly ingrained habits.

Overcoming does not mean suppressing! Overcoming means to look at the wrong inclination, to question it, to weigh the why and wherefore in order to recognize and discard what is not good. What is important here is also our personal goal. *For what* do I want to let it go?

Let us remember the following: Over time, all negative feelings, thoughts, words and actions become imprinted in the subconscious. By thinking and behaving in the same way over and over again, they take root deeper and deeper in our body cells. It is necessary to work off this imprinting.

Many people affirm the existence of their soul, which pulsates in the physical body. But we people hardly know the language of our soul.

Rarely do we hear our soul; we believe it to be a mute being in us.

Nothing, but absolutely nothing, in our existence is mute! Every sunbeam is a revelation of God. The radiations of all the planets are words of life. Every inconspicuous blade of grass is a symphony from the consciousness of the *I Am*. Every animal, whether large or small, radiates the life from God's All-life and feels that the creative power pulsates in it.

In contrast, the human being is dulled, also with regard to his soul. We people usually look only at the shell, the body, at matter, also at the shells of animals and plants. We do not realize what is going on in them.

Since the Fall of the divine beings, the fine substance condensed and became matter. On the way to condensation, the shell of the soul, the human being, and its three-dimensional world came into being.

We generally speak of "matter." However, matter is not all alike! There is a finer matter and a coarser and a very coarse matter.

People who live more and more in the omnipotence of God, in the love for God and neighbor, realize that their true being pulsates in them, the heavenly being. Such a material body is much finer.

Generally speaking, the consistency of the human material body changes as a result of a person's orientation toward the divine in his soul. With an increasing devotion to the Divine, the physical body gradually becomes finer. The structure of a person who has only recently begun to strive to draw closer to his true being can therefore still be characterized as "coarser."

Coarser and denser is above all the matter of those people who have turned away from God through their wrong way of thinking and acting. Coarse—which means very condensed, up to nearly bursting density—is the person who acts brutally, aggressively and destructively toward people and the animal and plant world.

How do human beings find the way to the language of their soul?

For one thing, the love for God and neighbor wants to reach our body through our soul. For another, our soul also wants to be heard by us, the human being.

If our conscious mind and subconscious are still very burdened, then the particles of the soul are also correspondingly darkened. Despite the different degrees of light and shadow, the soul tries to reach us.

We can hear it by means of our feelings, because the feelings are, as it were, the switching point between the soul and the physical body. The soul makes itself noticeable over the sounding board, "feeling."

The soul does not have thoughts. It has no words. It communicates via the corresponding moods that the events of the day bring with them.

The moods that run through us every day are quite different, depending on what we see, hear, smell, taste or touch. During the day, we experience that impulses reach our level of feelings externally via the senses. The soul responds via feelings and expresses itself in the corresponding moods.

In the early morning, when we awaken, our soul already makes itself known. A mood develops through our feelings. Either we are in a good or a bad mood. We are happy or we are angry. One person is sad, the other frightened or worried.

First of all, everything is based on attunement or moods. They come from the soul via the level of feelings. So already upon awakening, our soul speaks to us. The moods first have their images. If we allow the images to become clearer to us, we may learn in our thoughts what is important for today.

The soul has spoken to us.

Dreams can also convey moods to the subconscious and conscious mind.

Often we downplay our dreams: "Well, that was nothing but a dream"—yet everything, absolutely everything, wants to tell us something! Especially if the dream leaves behind moods.

If a dream is still "there," that is, if the images of a dream are still present, then we notice certain moods that come to us from the dream.

The dream itself is mostly symbolic, just as everything we do is ultimately a symbolic language. The dream is also a symbol. It has images that can be composed of different situations. But the mood comes from a particular aspect of the dream, and that aspect may be a help for the day.

A mood from the dream becomes thoughts and images if we let this happen. If, when this mood comes out of the dream, we endeavor to let it come in the morning, to let it rise, then this mood comes into our thoughts, and we know approximately what it wants to tell us. But it also comes in images during the day and shows us again what the dream wanted to signal to us; it is quite different, but a dream is often composed of different situations, and one situation brings about a mood.

Even morning pains can trigger certain moods. So we should take time to explore what our moods are trying to convey to us, through our subconscious and our conscious mind.

The following applies at every moment:
Christ in us is our Helper.

The level of feelings shows us already in the morning and throughout the day what is going on in our soul particles and in our subconscious and conscious mind: joy or sorrow, fear or worry, inhibitions or compulsions.

Thus, our feelings convey to us in moods the message for the day. The feelings, the message from the soul, may be very pressing under certain circumstances, especially when a so-called "uneasy" feeling develops in the solar plexus in the central nervous system. This is often an admonishment and a wake-up call from the soul.

It is vitally important to know that from our soul particles and from our subconscious and conscious mind, only that comes to light, which the individual has previously thought of and attributed to these three components, soul, subconscious and conscious mind.

Even our wrong actions, everything we do that does not correspond to our true nature, comes from the soul and reveals itself in corresponding moods.

We ourselves have input every mood—no matter what images and thoughts it produces. The soul communicates because it wants to free itself from the all-too-human, from the sinful aspects.

Everything that comes out of our soul, positive or negative, is ultimately we ourselves. We ourselves first entered it into the conscious mind. Unless the negative input is recognized and cleared up very soon, it entrenches itself in the subconscious and darkens the particles of our soul.

The so-called "pangs of conscience" also reach us from the level of feelings.

The conscience also has moods. There is, for example, the fear of something—we do not yet know what it is, but we feel anxiety; we feel threatened; we feel driven; we feel that we have said or even done something that not only burdens us, but could possibly become dangerous.

We are prompted by our soul to break down the moods in the conscious mind, to look at the thoughts that are developing, to figure out what needs to be remedied.

The broken-down pangs of conscience also help us to feel remorse and to overcome with Christ what is not good. Among other things, they help us to recognize possible dangers in time and to counter them effectively. In each case, it is important that we change our way of thinking and no longer think, say and do the same and similar things.

Even if we are frightened by something or if people say something to us that startles us, if our blood boils and our mood changes, then we can be sure: Our soul is sending its signals.

The mood shows itself either in images or thoughts.

Flared up feelings or dejection are also moods that have certain contents.

Many a person thinks, "In this day and age, we cannot afford to have feelings."

Feelings, however, have nothing to do with "sentimentalism," which is based on self-pity and disparagement of one's neighbor. Those who turn off their feelings also turn off their conscience.

Over time, people who ignore this level become so-called monsters who denigrate others solely to move their personal aspects, their ego, into the foreground. In doing so, they often maneuver cleverly and always for their own sake. To be against others always means to be self-serving for oneself, for one's all-too-humanness, for one's ego. This may give the individual temporary advantages—but no one has ever become happy, truly happy, through this in the long run.

The feeling is the link to the soul. And Christ gives impulses via feelings. For example, we feel something, but we do not yet know what exactly we are feeling, but this feeling enters our world of thoughts. If we ask, "What is in my thoughts?" and ask Christ for help, then an impulse comes from the very basis of the soul. Pictures open in us, more thoughts open, and we know what lies behind our thoughts. The more we explore what is going on underneath in us and clear it up and stop doing it, the more our consciousness expands and we learn to understand our neighbor. But when the level of feelings is "closed off," the neighbor will not be understood, quite the opposite.

Thus, we could indeed ask the question: Who is between soul and person? Who is blocking the level of feelings, the link to the soul and to Christ?

On the one hand, it is we ourselves, by building a huge wall. We hear the laws of life again and again; we know about the Ten Commandments of God; we know about the teachings of Jesus, the Christ; but we do not start to actualize, step by step. It is not that we should have actualized everything overnight, no, but we should take the steps, each day, to Christ in us. Then the feeling and the sensation become more and more alive, and we learn what we should clear up in order to grow closer to Him and also to understand our neighbor. Then the assertiveness dissolves, and justice moves in; for the feeling weighs, and the sensation measures. Therefore, this means that a so-called uneasy feeling comes, and we realize: Something has arrived here that wants to tell us something. If we clear up our all-too-human aspects, our sinfulness, and if we no longer do it, then we have access to our level of feelings. We have access to Christ in us. If we don't do that, then we build a blockade. And this blockade can be a wall between soul and human being. Then we are a monster, so to speak—we just lash out.

We realize how important the feeling in us is, the door to life, to Christ—and also from Christ to us.

The Christ Telephone—
a Hotline for "Please" and "Thank You"

From a teaching hour with Gabriele
on December 1, 2006

Especially in our time, when turbulences are coming, one after the other, the Spirit of God calls and gives us help upon help, but He also admonishes: "Save yourself, whoever wants to be saved, before this world passes away!"

An exhortation, a wake-up call, because in all generations, humankind has sinned gravely against the Mother Earth. It is against the Spirit of God, against Mother Earth. Until today, the escapades of the human ego have inflicted untold suffering on Mother Earth.

People have rarely listened to the word of God; but the Admonisher, God, our Father in Christ, has been and is always present. He knocks in us. He knocks in our conscience. He calls us by way of the Ten Commandments that He gave us through Moses. He calls us through the teachings of Jesus, the Christ. His love does not let up; His love is infinitely great.

Jesus, the Son of God, became our Redeemer on the cross at Golgotha. The redeeming power is in each of us. When we become quieter, aware that the innermost being is not of this world, then every now and then we feel the pulsebeat of infinity. It is the heart of the soul, it is the knocking of the loving eternal Father who is calling us through Christ, our Redeemer.

Many people know: Christ in us.
But many a one asks:
"Well, where is Christ? How can I reach Him?"
How is it when we want to talk to our neighbor? We are used to picking up the phone, to pulling the mobile phone out of our pocket, or rushing to the computer, or otherwise trying to contact our neighbor. It has become a habit: I can talk to my fellow people at any time.

But talking to Christ, is however still "abstract" for many. That is why there are many exercises for meeting Christ in us—of course, whoever wants to!

One suggestion from the Kingdom of God is that those who truly seek to draw closer to Christ pick up the "spiritual receiver," to speak to Him.

Where is the receiver?
How then, can we speak to Christ?
Many of us know that near our heart is the "Christ-center," the Christ-light that illuminates and flows through the spiritual centers, the centers that are inherent in us: the Order, the centers of Will, Wisdom, Earnestness, of Patience, Love and Mercy. There is an energetic current flowing in us that is always present, that flows through our breath, that brightens our cells, that pulsates in our soul.

As stated, we are used to picking up the phone so we can talk to our neighbor.

The Kingdom of God teaches us: "Christ in us."

We know that near our heart, that is, in our chest, is the central place of the Christ of God. Let us call this central place the "receiver," the spiritual receiver. Let us pick up this spiritual receiver more often!

Let us try it out:
We place our right hand on our chest.

Here is the central light; here is the spiritual receiver; here we can speak to within, into our inner being.

Here is the Christ-center, the switchboard of Christ that hears us, that receives our deep requests, our conversations. And Christ in us gives us answer.

But we do not hear Him yet. Why not? Do we need a phone number? No. But we need the increasing fulfillment of the Ten Commandments of God and of the teachings of Jesus, the Christ.

So that we perceive and feel that He is actually present, we should get into the habit of picking up the receiver more often, the "spiritual receiver," the center of the Christ of God.

When we pray, we should resolve to pray to within. When we pray, let us get into the habit of first placing our hand on the Christ-center, on the center that hears us, that hears everything.

Let us think deeply into the Christ-center:
"Christ in me." With this, we pick up the receiver. We call Him.

Each one of us can, when we get hectic, for example, quickly go the Christ-center and pick up the receiver: "Christ in me." No matter where we are, we can quickly place our right hand on the Christ-center through our jacket: "Christ in me."

The next step would be that during a conversation with our neighbor we also first silently speak into ourselves: "Christ in me"—and then further: "Christ in my neighbor."

We often meet a lot of people, hectic people. Many negative thoughts often come up in us as well. Let us practice: "Christ in me." The moment we earnestly think "Christ in me," we become gentler. Suddenly we feel pangs of conscience and we say to ourselves: "We cannot think like that about our neighbor or even talk to him like that!"

If we start a conversation, and we know we're going to meet people who aren't exactly well-disposed toward us, then we shouldn't begin right away, but should very briefly turn aside or quickly place our hand on the Christ-center, "Christ in me"—very briefly. We can briefly place our hand on our chest, that's not a problem.

What is important is: "Christ in me—and Christ in all those with whom I now have a conversation." Let us pause and go briefly within, and then start talking and we will suddenly feel: Something is happening in us. Before, we might have thought, "I'm really going to tell him off now!"—And now we say, "Yes, I will say it plainly and clearly," but our words will be completely different. They have taken on weight, power; it is the Spirit of God whom we have called.

When the family gets together, and when things perhaps get quite hectic, when some people want to argue or we ourselves are indignant about something and are quarrelsome: Let us very quickly put our hand on the Christ-center. The "Christ-switch" always hears our sincere request for help: "Christ in me—Christ in my neighbor—Christ in all family members—Christ in me."

Let us feel to within! Then we enter a conversation, or a family gathering, we then go to the table. And we will feel that something is happening in us. Suddenly we feel that we formulate things differently, that we speak differently, that totally different words come—It is the Spirit of God that is helping us. And if we sometimes "fall out" of our inner being, that's not so bad either. We have pangs of conscience that say: "Well, this and that are waiting to be cleared up."

And what happens thereby?

Some people feel a pulsation in themselves. Christ wants to communicate with us. But there is still so much turbulence in our brain. If, with Him, we endeavor to reduce this turbulence, what the day brings as all-too-human aspects—we also say, the sinfulness—to recognize and clear this up, and to become ever more aware of the commandments of God and the teachings of our Redeemer, then we become calm, the turbulence fades away. We feel more secure; we live more consciously; we breathe more deeply. Joy and thankfulness move into us. We experience something we may have merely been abstractly addressing until now: Christ in us.

We call Him. We take the spiritual receiver in hand. We talk to Him; we pray to Him. And we resolve for this exercise:

"Christ in me!—Christ in my neighbor!"

No matter where we meet people, no matter with whom we talk—at work, in the family, in the enterprises—there is hustle and bustle everywhere, but One is there who is security and tranquility:

"Christ in me!—Christ in my neighbor!"

We are used to holding on to something, even if it is the telephone receiver. And here we also hold firmly to the central listener, to the universal listener, to the center of the Christ of God, to the center of our being, to the switching point for our spiritual current.

Those who want to, join in.

And we feel: He does not leave us alone.

"Save yourself, whoever wants to be saved, before this world passes away!"—a call of the heart from God, our Father, to us, who wants to press us to His heart and to whom we find our way through Christ, our Redeemer.

Learn to Live with Nature and the Animals, then You Will Learn to Understand Yourself and Your Neighbor Better

From a seminar of the same name with Gabriele on March 3, 2001

In order to learn to better understand ourselves, we first question what "responsibility" means to us. For many people, the word "responsibility" is merely a term, something abstract that concerns them only theoretically, as it were. Therefore, it does not bother them much when they hear that before the law of God, they are responsible for all their thinking, speaking and doing.

If we realize that all feelings, sensations, thoughts, every word, indeed, all our behavior, is energy and that no energy is lost, it is a logical conclusion that there must be a reaction to every action. However, this is not just an abstract rule, a truth, that our intellect affirms, and it does not apply just generally to our world as a whole. Rather, the chain of actions and reactions is the reality of our personal lives on Earth.

All of us act unceasingly; we send out feelings, sensations, thoughts; we speak; we act. According to the content of our actions, we cause this or that for which we are and remain responsible. And every action that goes out from a person comes back to them as a reaction; it goes into their soul and cell structure as an energetic record and is stored as an input in the cosmos. Thus, each one of us bears the responsibility for what we do or do not do, as well as for our inaction with regard to the divine laws accepted by us.

How often do we say "I want ..."—and yet do not do it. For instance: "I want to live with my fellow people and with nature and the animals," but many do not want the resulting work on ourselves, the implementation of the laws of God, which are our true life.

"We want ..." or "I want ..." means: We have realized that what we declare as our intention needs to be done by us. But we should not leave it at that!

As the saying goes: "The road to hell is paved with good intentions." What is meant is precisely those good insights that we follow up with the words "I want …" with the resolution, but still do not follow through with it in our lives. Thus, the word "want," like the word "responsibility," has become an elastic term that everyone interprets for themselves personally in the way that is currently to their advantage.

The following remarks on the topic "Learn to live with nature and animals, then you will learn to understand yourself better and also your neighbor" are addressed to those who are not content with the resolution, with the realization of what actually should be done, but have decided to set a new course in their lives.

If we want to live in the right way with our fellow people and with nature, then we must first become aware that life is divine communication. Everything we see and what we do not see is life. All infinity, all pure forces and pure forms are filled with the life that is God. On the other hand, the Earth and everything that lives in it, on it and above it, including the material universe, are merely a reflection of infinity, merely a reflection of the Being. The primordial image is the Being; it is the life. The reflection, the mirror image, contains the life.

The kingdoms of nature, we human beings, all souls in the purification planes, all material and finer-material heavenly bodies are therefore mere reflections of the Being. The density, matter and the finer-material heavenly bodies on which souls live are merely permeated and are carried by the life, God. This happens via the incorruptible and therefore indestructible core of life in our soul, which is surrounded by the condensed life form, the human being. By means of the core of life or core of being, the connection to God, the one source of life, is made.

Consequently, in all of infinity, everything pure as well as the central core, the core of being in the soul of every human being, is in communication with each other. The material cosmos, the purification planes with the souls, all human beings, the nature kingdoms, all plant and animal species, all minerals in liquid and solid form are a part of density, which consists of various degrees of density.

Life is unity, also called All-communication; it is the All-Spirit, which unites all that is pure through the All-communication.

The kingdoms of nature know no separation from the All-Spirit. They are connected and feel connected with the great All-One, who unites them and with whom they are one.

Life, the All-communication, also knows no death. Let us become aware that all material forms of nature—for example, the trees, the bushes, the flowers—know no death.

For nature, the dying of the external form is nothing other than the discarding of a temporal form to again be in the true, the original form of consciousness. The same is true for the animals. They do not know "death." When they discard their temporal form, which I would like to also call the earthly garment, then they are what they are in their consciousness: state of consciousness that became form. Stones, too, all the minerals, solid and liquid, know no death. No matter how their external form is abused and changed by human beings—they remain the state of consciousness in the All-Spirit.

However, nature and animals are afraid of people because in many ways they force them in often bestial ways to die unnaturally. Many people kill without thinking about life and who it is that has given life to nature and animals. The wanton and deliberate killing of the plant and animal world is an intrusion in the harmonious flow, in the All-communication, in life.

The intrusions in the communication of life are recorded in the depiction of all the events on Earth in the atmospheric chronicle, for instance, the cutting down of trees filled with sap, or the wanton trampling and destruction of plants of all kinds, or even the manipulation of groups of plants, or allowing hundreds of thousands of animals to suffer, the killing, also the deliberate trampling of animals, torturing them and depriving them of their species-appropriate life, and much, much more.

The countless intrusions in the life of the nature kingdoms reach back to the beginning of the condensation, to the Fall-event. On the one hand, these unlawful actions were adopted by more and more people and, on the other hand, by many animal species, which, via the atmospheric chronicle, were and are stimulated by human beings to kill.

The programs of negative behavior created by human beings were therefore transferred to the animals. Human beings are the perpetrators; they bear the responsibility, that is, the guilt, for this. They burdened and burden themselves—not the animal. If therefore, animals often hunt and consume the weakest of their animal brothers and sisters, then nevertheless, this happens solely through a millennia-long influence on the part of human beings. Therefore, this degeneration came about by way of human beings and corresponds neither to the All-life nor to a natural way of dying, as provided for in the laws of nature.

Despite everything that was and is done to the animals, our animal brothers and sisters are much more species-appropriate, and in their behavior, ethically and morally higher than human beings. The human being as a human abnormality, can be called killer and tormentor. For example, he cruelly tortures male and female cattle for his benefit and profit in order to prepare the coerced life force for artificial insemination, which he then carries out.

Farms that keep animals artificially inseminated by people as "fattening animals" for meat production are nothing more than production sites of artificial life that is killed after a certain time—determined by the farmer—so that people can feast on an animal carcass.

Let us realize that the animals that were and are created by people via artificial insemination to end up on the slaughtering block are also living beings. However, God, the Eternal, the All-Spirit, does not give life to the animals that are created by people in their self-will; instead, the human beings gave and give them a part of their own life force. Human beings interfered with the law of nature and purloined the carrier substance of life, in order to produce with it, for example, animals that are intended for wanton killing. With this, human beings play themselves up as creators. However, since humankind is not the creator of infinity, the existence of every artificially produced animal is attached to the life-battery of all those involved with this, including the people who consume the flesh of their animal brothers and sisters, that is, the consumers.

People who condone, carry out and support such inhuman acts on animals are callous and unconscionable. They hold high the flag of their ego principle, which is, "I am my own best friend." One day they will be chained to their flagpole. What then?

With the countless patterns of behavior against the divine law of unity, which include all the energies of feeling, sensing, thinking and speaking, humankind has created its individual cycle. It revolves only around itself, according to the principle: "Everything serves me!"

The cycle of ego is not integrated in the All-cycle of life. People in this narrow ego-awareness have disconnected from the All-communication. They cultivated and cultivate only their limited communicative ego. The personal cycle, the ego cycle, is thus solely oriented to the body, to the carnal. It starts from the inputs in the conscious mind and the subconscious, that is, from the brain, via the similarly stored, that is, burdened, body cells and physical functions and returns to the conscious mind and the subconscious. This is directed among other things by the person's inputs into the corresponding repository planets. The thought of the immortal soul and of the communication with the All-life was thereby lost. The consequence of this is that people are largely concerned only with themselves and their interests. Their personal well-being, their welfare and their being appreciated are in the foreground. This is what they then call life.

How does the personal cycle develop? In short, it goes like this: Every human being has an immortal soul that contains the incorruptible core of being, which is divine. The core of being is in the All-communication with God, the life, thus, with infinity, with all pure forces and forms and with the life *in* the material nature kingdoms, and with this, also with the core of being in all human beings. Shells formed around the incorruptible core of being as a result of negative behavior patterns. The external, dense, very much coarsened shell, that is, the coarse material, is the carnal, the human being.

From the head of the human being, from his inputs into the brain against life, these shells came into being.

These shells originated from the person's head, from his inputs into the brain against life. First the person stored and stores in his conscious mind and his subconscious. What he has stored in the brain is gradually transferred to the whole body. The inputs go into the cell structure and influence all the functions of the human body. The spiritual particle structure of the soul also absorbs these inputs. From this result the energetic shells, which are the direct radiation of the human being. His behavior is then according to this as well.

As mentioned, the person also stores his personal inputs in the corresponding stars and planets of the material cosmos and the immaterial cosmos, the purification planes. These human predispositions are of a personal nature. They do not have access to the All-communication, which is impersonal, that is, lawful.

Because of this, the ego-type—the one more, the other less—leads an isolated existence, through which he has lost the connection with his fellow human beings, with nature and with the animals. We can compare a personal cycle with a spider's web. The spider catches a fly in its web. The person has created a "spider's web" for himself, as it were, and has also caught himself in it. This has led to blunted feelings and a blunted conscience in such a person. He possibly has contact only with like-minded people; he rejects everything else that does not fit into his narrow, ego-centered cycle of feelings and thoughts.

People without a true sense of life and a conscience think and act like robots. With their behavior patterns, they often destroy everything that is not profitable for them. They do not consider the life of their fellow people, let alone the life of nature and animals and of the Mother Earth.

As stated, their ego-principle is: "I am my own best friend. Everything serves me for my wellbeing." They do not care if nature and animals suffer under this. For them, everything is just a thing, if anything, without life. Everything should benefit solely them, even if it is the life of the animals and nature.

I repeat: People who ruthlessly maaintain their personal cycle have separated themselves from the

All-communication. They are merely maintained by the core of being in their soul. This lack of feeling leads to a monster-like behavior that destroys and kills for its own sake. Mother Earth with her diverse plant species, with her animals and minerals is at the mercy of such types of people.

With unprecedented clarity, the current generation of people is proving that merely talking about protecting biodiversity and protecting the animal kingdom is of no use. Even when many a so-called nature lover reports about the beauty of nature and about the animal world, for example, about its manifold splendid colors and the markings of its feathers or pelts, this amounts to nothing. Just a person's word is of little use if it is not borne by concern and help for our second neighbors, our brothers and sisters in nature, the trees, bushes, grasses, flowers and animals. When we speak of the nature kingdoms, we must not forget the minerals, nor the elemental forces, the soil, the water, the wind, the fire, also the sun and the other stars and planets—everything is part of the All-unity, love and wisdom of God, who is also the Spirit of nature and of the elements.

In all honesty: How often have we walked or do walk through the woods, over meadows or along a beautifully winding country lane, and thought or said, in effect: "It is so beautiful in the woods, in nature! The tranquility is so good for me. The singing, twittering and joyousness of the birds is good for the disposition." Or we marvel at the mighty, ancient trees that endure wind, storm, cold and heat and still grow and bear the fruit of their species.

Or we see deer agilely leaping over tufts of grass or small trees, or hares, foxes, wild boars, or the nimble, dainty squirrels whose coats glow wonderfully in the element of fire, in the sun.

We think and say how beautiful and soothing it all is. But what do *we* drag along with us into the woods, over the meadows and on the pathways through the fields?—ultimately, our worries and problems, our gray radiation, which we silver-plate with nice words, for example, how beautiful and soothing it all is. Once we have finished our walk, we think or say how nice and relaxing the walk was. Perhaps we then talk about it again the next morning, when we talk about how we spent our Sunday.

A little later, we hardly remember it, because we are again preoccupied with ourselves, with what we also took along during the walk: our gray, often gloomy, ego-self.

Perhaps we see and hear on television or read in the daily newspaper how animals—which, basically, are also beings of freedom—are kept in barns, how animals are bred for meat production, what animals get to eat, how they are held in animal transports, how they are treated, killed and dismembered in slaughterhouses or how they have to eke out their existence, abused and tortured in animal experiments, until they are delivered by death. Perhaps we then say: "That is terrible!"

We see, hear and read a lot. How do we act? On the one hand, we think and say: "How beautiful nature is; it has given us a lot"—on the other hand, we think and say: "How terrible," in view of the suffering of the animals, which is plainly shown to us on television or in press reports. Mostly it stays with such and similar comments. Who even thinks about any similar wrongdoing in themselves, in order to change some of it?

Perhaps we have some good advice in mind, on how others should act. And how do we act?

Do we communicate with the little bird that is building its nest for its young in spring, that expresses its joy in song and jubilation, which is due to the Creator?

Do we hear the Creator's language deep in our soul from the incorruptible core of being by way of the world of birds?

Do we hear the Creator's language through the mighty old trees, through shrubs and flowers? Deep in our soul, do we hear what the fox, the deer, the hare, the wild boar or the graceful squirrel transmit to us?

Do we hear the All-Spirit, the life, in the stone?

Do we hear the language of the wind, of the fire, of water and of the Mother Earth?

Do we grasp what a ray of sunlight wants to tell us?

Do we hear the lamentation of the enslaved animals deprived of their freedom, in the animal transports and in the animal testing facilities?

Do we feel the plight of the animals on the farms that I call production facilities for the slaughtering blocks, that were artificially procreated to then be killed for self-interest?

Do we hear and feel the cries and fears of the animals in the slaughterhouses, slaughtered to be an animal carcass for human beings and their cravings?

One day, countless souls or people will have to answer the following questions before the judge, the law of sowing and reaping: Who gave you the authority to create life artificially and to wantonly kill living beings? Who gave you the right to disregard life, so that things go well for you?

If we think only about what was mentioned here very briefly, let alone about what else people cruelly cause to animals, then this can be expressed in one statement: The human monster has no feeling and no conscience anymore; it becomes more and more brutal and inventive when it comes to destroying the living beings and life forms of nature. While doing so, it doesn't realize that it is destroying itself. Because it is as it is, in general, it can quite rightly be said that in its thinking and behavior, the human being consists only of itself. The incorruptible core of being deep in the soul of every human being is enveloped by the offenses against life.

Those who still have some feeling and a conscience will reorient themselves; they will no longer leave it at nice words about the walk in nature and will no longer be content with the words "how terrible!" when they see, hear and read how their little brothers and sisters, the animals, are suffering or when their brothers cut down trees full of sap or when whole forests are wiped out by huge fires.

How do we get back to the All-communication? How do we experience the All-Spirit, the life that speaks to us from countless degrees of consciousness in nature, from the plant, animal and mineral kingdoms? What must be done to merge into the All-communication, into the life, to protect life, to preserve and become one with life?

We can learn and practice to find our true self, the All-communication, the life, and its language of consciousness. We should get out of the habit of taking the word "want" or "we should" as an excuse, as a pretext, which the deed does not follow. There is no excuse before the law of sowing and reaping, if we know how we should behave as sons and daughters of God.

The excesses of our generation including their consequences show that God does not conform to us. We must change, in order to draw closer to Him. We must take the first step toward the All-communication, and then the Eternal One will come toward us.

The first step toward the All-communication is to make use of each day, which is an aspect of our life on Earth, in order to become free of our spiritual and physical burdens. This is done by exploring and questioning our pessimistic, derogatory, that is, negative, thoughts, our undisciplined and inept speech, with which we merely want to enhance ourselves. We do this by asking ourselves whether our thoughts are with our work, or to where they go, or what is cavorting around in our world of feelings, and much more.

We have to learn to take our life on Earth in hand, which day after day shows itself through our feelings, thoughts, words and actions, also through our soliloquies, our monologues, the mental arguments with our neighbor, which are nothing other than the fight of our ego against him.

Each day, we experience aspects of our personal inputs, we experience ourselves. By questioning all that occupies us—which usually takes place in soliloquies and accusations of others—we experience a part of our inputs, which is a revelation of our human self.

The second step is to clear up what is burdening us with the power of the Spirit of God in us.

The third and essential step is now to stop thinking and doing the same thing, that is, to restrain ourselves.

The fourth step is to work out a divine principle of the law from the negative things we have worked on, whereby the Commandments of God and the Sermon on the Mount of Jesus help us do this. We should repeatedly make ourselves aware of the divine principles that we have worked out; we should jot them down as a reminder, and put the note in a place where we often spend time.

Only once the principle of the law of life has been absorbed by our brain cells, will we fulfill it as a matter of course, because the principle of the law or the principles of life fulfilled by us have gained space in the consciousness of every cell of our body, thus shaping our body and also entering our soul.

This means that the dark shadows that once polarized and burdened our body and soul have been transformed into light and power by the Spirit of God. Then light and power move into our soul and into our body. This also means that our envelopments, which enclose the incorruptible core of being, become lighter. Our body structure, which is a material vibration, becomes finer and our nature more balanced.

The next steps are to go within in order to attain calmness. From this, results the foresight and insight into the things of life and the deep perception in the observation of what surrounds us.

Let us be aware that to attain the All-communication, we have to live more consciously, so that we can gather positive energies, which we use for the deep contemplation of what is around us, for example, to experience the plants, the animals and the minerals, to gain the experience ourselves that everything lives and feels as we do.

Thus, life is All-communication.

Learn to Love,
Gain Freedom and Be Happy

From a teaching hour with Gabriele
on September 14, 1997

Learn to love—that's three words: Learn to love. In these words lies the whole path that each of us has to take to regain, step by step, our divine heritage, which is God's love. Let us remember the cardinal commandment: *"Love God with all your heart and with all your soul, with all your might, and your neighbor as yourself!"*

Three aspects of love: Love God, your neighbor, and yourself.

Many say it is a difficult path to love God with all our strength and in addition, to love our neighbor as we love ourselves. How we love ourselves is merely the steps toward love, but not yet our divine heritage, the stream of love in which all pure beings move.

The question to all of us now is: How do we love ourselves? After all, it is said that we should love our neighbor as we love ourselves. Often it comes to a sad analysis. We love ourselves to the extent that we rarely question whether what we think, speak and do is in accordance with God's love. For us, our thinking, speaking and acting is "objective," that is what we are, that is each of us ourselves.

Some people may say, "I don't love myself. That's not true of me." But let us ask ourselves: What about when one of our fellow people characterizes us, or perhaps criticizes us, saying, "I am contemptuous of you; you don't understand your occupation, your craft. You're not a socially acceptable person, you're immoral," or even, when he tells us outright, "You're bad!" How does this make us feel? How do we react? Do we remain calm, in the inner certainty that we rest in God's love, which is not only viable, but simply *is*? Or do we remember certain situations; do we protest because we do not see ourselves as the other person does? What happens then?

When we protest, we have to say that we love our ego, we love ourselves more than we love the one who may have characterized us, who may have even wanted to help us thereby. Thus, we love ourselves more. Our neighbor merely stirred up our self-love, that is, our self-satisfied love, which we wanted to keep.

And then what happens when we react like that? We point the arrow at our neighbor because he presumes to characterize us—that is, to "criticize" us—and we have to admit that our self-love does not tolerate these "attacks." Why? Because we think we are better and wiser. This means that we love ourselves more than the one who characterized us. Is that the true love?

Thus, we have to learn to again become capable of love from within ourselves. Where does it start?—with forgiveness, by forgiving, with the cycle of clearing things up.

It is actually sad when we have to speak of the love for God and neighbor, since we are all children of the one love, children of the eternal Father, who beheld us in His heart, in His great primordial heart, and gave birth to us as beings of love out of His great primordial heart of love.

Many people speak of love, and it is nothing other than the longing for love, the longing for secureness. Where does the longing for love, for security, come from? Ultimately, from the very basis of our soul, because in the very basis of our soul, we are beings of love. In the very basis of our soul is the great love, God, the love that tirelessly knocks at our soul and at the gate that leads to the conscious mind of human beings.

We define this knocking of our innermost being, the knocking of God at the gate of our conscious mind, as a longing for love, as a longing for security. If we do not receive it, we call our neighbor unloving and possibly denigrate him because he does not give us what we long for. If we get a tinge of all-too-human love from our neighbor, then we are happy for a short time. But if the tinge of this human love fades, then we continue to long for love. In the process, we have shadowed ourselves more and more, because we constantly expect someone to give us the love that we long for and that ultimately is deep in our soul. Then we begin to act against our neighbor. We denigrate him; we expect from him what, in the end, he cannot give us either, because he has shadowed himself in a similar way as we have, since he is also looking for love. Both are looking for love.

Everyone is looking for love, and no human being can give us love. Why? Because each one is seeking it.

We have gotten into the habit of leaning on our neighbor, to perhaps elicit a spark of love. We have gotten into the habit of demanding from our neighbor. And many a one cannot even meet our demands at all because they can't give what we ask for. As a result, we human beings have become more and more selfish. And the word "selfish" bears within itself the addiction, the addiction to love, the addiction to security. This addiction always seeks to obtain from others what it does not have itself. As a result, the body of the individual has become heavier and heavier, heavy due to the many sinful, that is, negative, thoughts. We have lost our posture before our true being, which is love. We people lost our posture before God, our eternal Father, and before Christ, our Redeemer. And yet we long for love.

We despair of God because He does not give us what we want.—Well, then, what do we want?—

The transformed-down love, the self-love. He cannot give it to us at all because He does not have it.

We demand that God give us our sinful freedom, that He help us to distance ourselves from our neighbor, to reject him. He cannot do that because He does not have that.

We demand that He bring us a person who loves us—who loves us the way we want. He cannot do that, because He does not have selfish love.

So we reproach God many times for not giving us what we want. He cannot give it to us because He is not a sinner, but the great eternal love. And the eternal love never forsakes us!—Why? Because we are in His primordial heart as pure beings, eternally. Therefore, He calls and knocks at the gate to the conscious mind—and we humans do not understand Him, because we have burdened ourselves. We have turned away from our origin, from the love. We have transformed down our divine heritage into our ego heritage, namely, into our world of thoughts. And these our sinful thoughts, these our sinful words and actions are our personal heritage, which is our ego. And that is what we love, and it is from this that we want to be loved.

What does "learn to love" actually mean? Love means to first learn on ourselves. Everything that stirs us up tells us that we can learn from it, because it stirs up only a part of our personal sinful inputs; it is our egoistic love.

So this means that we love ourselves more than we love our neighbor, let alone God, because the moment our ego rebels we turn against our neighbor and reject him. As a result, the human body became ever heavier. We grew more negligent, thus losing the posture toward our true being and God.

Therefore, learning to love simply means: Look at yourself! The negligence is shown by the behavior of our body. Do we think that as pure beings before the countenance of God, we adopt a posture like this: We cross our arms before God. We cross our legs before God. We rest our head on our palm. We eat and shovel in the food God has given us. These are all signs of our own inputs.

If God were to sit before us like this, would God assume this posture before us? What would we say? There are so many little situations from which we can learn.

Or let us imagine that God is sitting with us at the table, supporting His elbow on the table, resting His head on the palm of His hand and shoveling food into it. Then we would say, "Impossible! That's supposed to be God?!" But we allow ourselves to do it. And why? Because we have not learned to question ourselves: What makes us so heavy that we conduct ourselves in this way? Just by taking up this posture, we would have to immediately say, "Attention! Why do I now have this posture?"

And we immediately realize that certain thoughts are taking place in us, negative thoughts, heavy thoughts, urging us into this posture. They are thoughts against the symphony, the lightness of infinite love, that is, thoughts against love.

We could learn just from our body posture; we could learn from ourselves who we are and with what we have turned away from God's love. We could see images and see ourselves in these images because we store pictorially. And then the question applies, "Well, what have I put into my thoughts, into my wanting?" Usually it is an expectation. We expect something from our neighbor—and if he does not give it to us, then we reject him and cross our arms, for example.

This is also a sign that we reject our neighbor and love ourselves more than we love the innermost part, the pure in our neighbor, which is also in us. All these external forms of conduct can help us to learn—to learn what separates us from the love, from our divine heritage.

If we are willing to learn, then over time we realize that we are leaning on our fellow people. Why do we lean on them, that is, why do we expect this and that from them, which we could ultimately do ourselves? Because our spiritual energy, the love-energy, becomes weaker and weaker. We grow lethargic. And the indolence, in turn, has an effect on our body. The effects are different postures of our physical body. We all know them, and each one has its peculiarities. But these peculiarities are always an expression of our wrong attitudes, and thus, an expression of our self-love.

Only once we learn to stop leaning on our neighbor, expecting of him what we could do ourselves, and when we do for our neighbor what we expect of him, do we gain respect for ourselves. Respect for ourselves means that our body gradually straightens up, negligence decreases, and we then also gradually gain respect for our neighbor. For what we recognize about ourselves concerning our wrongdoings and clear up with the help of the Spirit of the Christ of God and no longer do, expands our consciousness, and we feel our neighbor more and more. We then experience the positive sides of our neighbor in our heart, in our spiritual consciousness, which opens ever more because we clear up our sinful aspects, that is, we remedy the beam in our eye with Christ. Then suddenly we have access to our neighbor. We change. Our thoughts grow more light-filled, our words richer in spiritual content. We learn, in turn, from our neighbor because we learn to understand him. Thus, we find our way to our neighbor, even when he rejects us. We find access to his inner being because we no longer expect anything from him, but do what we can ourselves.

From this inner posture we learn to ask, by asking our neighbor for help with what we cannot do, be it on our job, be it in the family—we do not lose face when we ask our neighbor to help us where we need help.

Through this we become free. We are increasingly aware that God is helping us. We increasingly stand in this stream of love, which is our divine heritage. The result is that we grow happy. From this freedom, which is in God, flows happiness. Happiness is not just knowing that God is love, but it is the flow of love through the soul and through the person. That is the response of God, the response of love. And we are happy because we live in love, because we have found our way home with our thoughts, with our feelings, with our words and actions, home to our true being, home to the love. Love then flows through our thoughts. Love permeates our words. Love permeates our actions. And we are like a ladle that draws from love, from the stream.

"Learn to love" thus means to begin with ourselves. Small things, such as external behavior, help us to recognize what our self-love is, what we have learned and become accustomed to, which is the same as being far from God.

Part of self-love is, as stated, the habit of having expectations of our neighbor. We are usually in the habit of expecting our neighbor to do this or that for us. We always expect something. When we see one of our fellow people, thoughts come. And ultimately, we also expect something from the one we see and know; even if we disparage him in our thoughts, we expect something. We are constantly in an attitude of expectation. All this wants to tell us something.

When we approach our neighbor, we expect something. When we distance ourselves from our neighbor, we expect something from another. All this and much more tells us that we do not stand by God, but by our ego. And all this helps us to question ourselves.

If we have learned to love, then we no longer expect anything, and then we will often do for our neighbor what he expects from us, but only as much as we can give him, so that he may recognize himself in his expectation—but without words, instead, through recognition, through self-experience.

So let us recognize ourselves first in our expectations. We expect our neighbor to do this or that for us, even though we know we would have the time to do it ourselves, be it at work, at home, in the family; often these are small things. For example, the husband expects the wife to do this or that on time. The woman expects the husband to be home on time, and much more. This attitude of expectation says that we are not with our neighbor. Because if we are for and with our neighbor, then we will consult each other, and we know when the husband will be home, and whether the wife can do this or that on time today. There are many, many little things that need to be agreed upon. But we do this only when we really love, otherwise everything is just expectation.

In those aspects in which we have recognized and cleared up our all-too-human aspects, our sinfulness, our spiritual consciousness expands. And from this, our own experience of clearing things up, we can then give an aspect of love. Therefore, our consciousness expands by clearing up our sinfulness, and as we clear it up, we can also draw from love and give. This does not mean that we must first become completely pure to be able to give—no: We can draw and give from our own experience. But the more we clear up sinful aspects, the greater the love for God and neighbor in us becomes. A sign that we have grown closer to the love is that we are much happier when the other person is better off than we are.

Then the question arises: Have I made my neighbor happy from my heart? Have I made my neighbor a little bit happier?—Because if my neighbor is better off than I am, I should be happy. These are the small things or the steps toward the love that expects nothing, that gives because it possesses everything.

When asked how we can, figuratively speaking, avoid "pointing arrows at our neighbor," Gabriele explained:

With the inputs from our past we react in the present—because we can react only with our inputs. Our correspondences, our ego, which is agitated, tells us what we have input. This is part of our sinfulness.

If we clear it up with the help of the Christ of God, and if we no longer do it—if we consciously no longer do it—then we clear out the negativity from our vessel, from the person and the soul, and the love for God and neighbor can flow more intensively and help and support us.

So we should first look at ourselves: What is our basis? Why is our ego agitated? If we clear up our ego and firmly resolve not to do this anymore, indeed, if we even write down the positive sides, the spiritual principles, when similar things come up, so that we immediately keep to the spiritual principles, to God's love, then we become more sensitive, then this learning gradually stops. We have then created a seismograph that is in the subconscious and in the conscious mind, but also in our soul, that immediately says, "Stop, look at yourself!" The seismograph that has been activated—it is an aspect of the Divine in us—immediately warns us and says, "Here you are wrong! Here you are against the commandment, against love!" And if we clear it up and no longer do it, the seismograph becomes ever greater, we grow more sensitive for the divine impulses. This is the clearing out of the ego, so that the great, powerful *I Am*, the love, our true being, the innermost being, breaks through more and more. Then we become free, steadfast in God and happy, because those who have found their way home, who have found their way home in themselves, are happy because they are secure in God.

We have now been talking about us human beings. But let us also consider the following:

Merely by considering an animal as a thing and withholding their love and help from it are people against God and against themselves. How much more does it affect us when we are against people? And what about all of nature, which we humans torture and maltreat? Here we are against God and against ourselves.

Or how often do we refuse to help our neighbor because we do not live in the present, because we constantly brood about our past and thereby merely reinforce it? Because with all these inputs that we deal with and that are our past, we react in the present. Each of us must at some point learn to live in today, not in what was yesterday. Yesterday, the past, comes into our present step by step, so that we can recognize it and clear it up with the help of the Christ of God and no longer do it. Only when we resolve the past, is the sinful gone; it remains as a memory. But we can draw from this memory, so that we can give the Divine. We will then, when we work through our past, not lose our memory; on the contrary, we will live more consciously.

So let us also think of the animals. Let us think of Mother Earth. How do we behave toward our second neighbors, toward the animals, toward all of nature? And finally: How do we behave toward God and toward our neighbor?

Reincarnation and Rebirth in the Spirit

From a teaching hour with Gabriele on January 15, 1988

The question is asked again and again: Where did we come from, where are we going?

We came from the origin, from God; we will go back to the origin in God. But what is in between? Incarnations—or only one incarnation? We determine this ourselves through our thinking, speaking and acting. It is said: As the tree falls, so will it lie. If we should pass on today, we are the same same as we were in the earthly garment. We take light and shadow with us into the realms of the beyond.

For many of us, death is still something uncanny because we can look only at matter and cannot penetrate space and time. Many believe that when the body dies, everything is over. Jesus of Nazareth said: "What a person sows, that he will reap"—

sowing and reaping! What do we sow, when do we sow, where do we sow, where is the field in which the seed sprouts? When does it sprout? In this life or in the spheres of purification? Or do we come back with the seed and it first sprouts in this or in another life? This is something we should think about.

For us human beings, death is something unpleasant. The body, which was once full of life, suddenly lies inert—the life has slipped away. The Kingdom of God sees it differently. The spirit beings see our earthly garment as a cloak—for one the cloak is too tight, it takes him longer to "undo the buttons" and slip out, for the other it is easier to take it off. The Kingdom of God views this similarly.

Therefore, this means that the soul clings to the body, and therefore, the cloak, the body, is often too tight. It adheres to the body, it adheres with all its fibers to matter, and when the hour comes, it can leave this body only with great difficulty. Why? Because it may still be carrying many burdens.

Let us think of a tethered balloon: If there is a lot of ballast in the basket, it pulls it down. If the ballast is thrown off, then it rises. It is similar with our soul. So what we sow today and do not clear up in time will sprout tomorrow. The seed goes into the field of the soul; the soul becomes heavy, earth-bound, and attaches itself to its body because it sees this as its life.

When asked by a participant why we are at all afraid of death, Gabriele replied:

The fear is there because we think, "What awaits us over there?" And what can we expect over there? Only what we are here. No more and no less awaits us over there than what we are here—and we are our thoughts, our words and our actions. We are speech, action, thought, feeling; passion or inner cheerfulness, selfless love, peace with our neighbor, harmony and happiness. Each day we can visualize how we will arrive on the other side. If we now close our eyes and do not open them anymore to matter, to this incarnation, then we will feel and think as a soul just as we did in the body. The closer we are to the Earth, the closer the soul is to matter. Then the soul does not get away from matter and may not even know that it has left the body. It remains among people and behaves as it did when it was a human being in the earthly garment.

This should make us think, because how quickly do we sow? When is the harvest? We can sow negatively today, and things go well for us all our life—the seed remains in the field of the soul. But the Spirit of God reminds us again and again that we repeatedly have the opportunity to make amends for many things in this life. We can also make amends in this life for what we caused in a previous life and what has not yet taken effect. We are led to situations about which we say, "What is happening here is none of my business; I cannot relate to it." Then why were we led there? Why are we witnessing a situation that seems like it doesn't concern us? In this life, we have never had anything to do with this person, and now we are experiencing firsthand a situation, a dispute, quarrel, or something else.

If we turn away and say, "It doesn't interest me, it's none of my business," then we have missed an opportunity. We were guided there to get impulses from the situation, so that we think about ourselves. Because the thoughts that come while two people are arguing, for example, tell us what we ourselves have to clear up, what lies in us. If we are alert, and clear up what comes to our mind based on the situation, then we may not have to bear a soul-debt from a past life, or it may be mitigated.

Therefore, at every moment we have the chance to transform our life, to reorient ourselves, to reflect on what we were thinking in this or that situation, that is, what we can clear up based on our thoughts.

At every moment, God's love and grace give us the possibility to find our way out of the law of sowing and reaping, also called the law of causality. We are not required to keep coming back, to keep going through new incarnations. This incarnation gives us the possibility not to come again, not to be drawn into an earthly garment. If we take advantage every day of these possibilities, these chances, then we will gradually feel what it means to attain rebirth in the spirit.

We can also attain and feel the rebirth in the Spirit of God while still on Earth. If our thoughts —no matter what situation we experience—are positive, if we see the positive over and over again and only address the negative so that our neighbor can gain insight; if we live in peace with our fellow people; if we have learned to love them, no matter what they say or do; if we no longer justify ourselves and disparage our neighbor, then we feel a flash of the Spirit of God in us and are placed in the power and strength of infinite grace and love. Only then are we happy from within because we are united with the cosmic forces.

Then we will no longer be afraid of so-called death—we look at ourselves, that is, each one looks at himself, at who he is. If we look at ourselves in the light of truth, then we are happy and in God, and death has no more fetters and barriers. However, if we are in the human being merely "as a human being," that is, if we think and feel all-too-humanly, that is, negatively; if we denigrate others so as to exhalt ourselves; if we defend ourselves; if we accuse; if we are spiteful, envious, quarrelsome, etc., then we also see ourselves this way—and we are afraid of death, because there is something in us that is saying, "Discard what you still are!" And we ignore that all too readily.

To the question of why people incarnate again and again and whether it can also be seen as a grace for the soul, since it can expiate its burden more quickly via the body, Gabriele answered:

Yes, that is correct. Here, for example, we endure an illness and thus expiate a burden. Through the illness, however, we do not know what we have caused. The cause flows out through an illness; we endure it, and when we accept it and thus turn to Christ, it is paid off in the soul.

When we accept a blow of fate and repent and make amends for what we have recognized, some things from past lives are erased in the soul. Thus, we realize how good it is that the past is covered up. If it were revealed to us while in the earthly garment, the chaos on this Earth would be much greater.

In the soul realms, we will not expiate our guilt—we also call it sin—through illness. There is no illness there; there, the images emerge; there, we see exactly what we have caused and this causes torment to the soul. We also see what our neighbor has done to us, and that we have paid him back in a similar way, and thus caused similar things.

If the soul cannot incarnate, there is only expiation, recognition, the experience through images, through remorse and the request for forgiveness. There, one can no longer make amends, but only ask for forgiveness. The soul has the help of the guardian beings; it has help through prayer and impulses from the Divine, because in every soul is also the Divine.

The soul has a much more refined sensation because it has discarded the material, heavy body. When the soul is incarnated, it feels more through the organism; in the soul realms, its sensations are more the discomfort, the suffering of the neighbor that it caused in the earthly garment—it is more the beholding and feeling the pain of the other.

Redemption in Us

From a teaching hour with Gabriele
on November 2, 2007

Ultimately, are not all of us seeking God? Many will say. "I wonder whether God exists." And many a one says: "I don't believe in God." ...

In all honesty, dear fellow people, we are all seeking peace; we are all seeking happiness; we are all seeking harmony. We all want to be loved. And many a person says, "Well, on this Earth, in this world, I haven't found any of this. I believed it now and then, but it was always a deception." But One never deceives us—it is truly God, our eternal, heavenly Father. His Spirit is in us. God, our eternal Father, sent His Son to us, Jesus, the Christ. He brought us redemption. Therefore, many will ask again, "Well, what does redemption mean? Are we redeemed at all? What did He redeem us from?" And many a church Christian will say, "Well, from our sins!"

Well, if Christ took away all our sins and takes them away at every moment, then we would have a perfect world. But each of us knows that we do not have a perfect world. Why? When each one observes himself: Is he whole? Is he satisfied? Is he happy in his heart? Is he joyful? Is he peaceful?

Few can say that—why? Because we call ourselves Christians and yet year after year we frequently merely say, "Jesus lives! Thy terrors now can, O death, no more appall us."

Words, words, dear fellow people, but Jesus said, *"Follow Me!"* And in His following it means: Do what I, that is, Jesus, the Christ, have commanded you!—If we do that, if we keep His commandments more and more each day, then the Redeemer-light in us grows ever greater. It becomes a mighty flame, and we feel that this great, mighty flame in us is the eternal Father's love through the Son, through the redeeming power. And over time, we realize that we get along with our neighbor. If we are against our neighbor, we suddenly feel that we can ask him for forgiveness, but that we can also forgive our fellow people when they are against us.

This is the beginning of the great love of the child for the Father. And this is truly the resurrection of the Christ of God in us. And it is our resurrection in Christ. If we merely say, "Jesus lives! Thy terrors now can, O death, no more appall us" as it says in a hymn, then we have to admit that the word "death" frightens us. Why does it frighten us?—because our thoughts are not in God, because our thoughts are sinful. But if we let Christ arise in our thoughts, in our feelings and words, in our actions, that is, deeds, then we feel what Jesus said in His farewell speech and repeatedly brought home to His apostles: *Love one another as I have loved you.* In the same way, Christ, our Redeemer, loves us as He promised us as Jesus of Nazareth.

Dear brothers, dear sisters, the love for God, our Father, the love for our neighbor and the love for nature is the resurrection in Christ. And in this way, the Redeemer-light, that is, Christ, can arise in us and we are united with Him. This is then the Good News. This is then the joy that we carry out aware that: "Yes, Christ lives in me; Christ is risen in my temple. And Christ lives through my thoughts, through my words and works. I am in Christ, and Christ is in me."

That is the Good News of love, that is the joy, which Christians should carry out into all the world, that which we daily experience ourselves: Christ in our words, Christ in our thoughts, Christ, the great Love and Mercy in us and through us. "*Love one another*," thus spoke the Lord, "*as I have loved you*."

If we do this, so that we truly become brothers and sisters, brothers and sisters in His Spirit, loving one another in His Spirit, then Christ is risen in us and we in Christ, because then we keep His commandments.

The love for God is the same as the love for neighbor. And only the love for God and neighbor enables us to overcome the ego. The love for God and neighbor is gentle and kind. It helps us get over our ego. It helps us to recognize and find the *I Am*, that is, the love for God and neighbor—if we take the trouble to compare our thinking and our whole behavior with the Ten Commandments of God and the Sermon on the Mount of Jesus of

Nazareth. Then we know where the ego blossoms and what we have to do so that the *I Am* can blossom.

How often did Jesus say to His apostles and disciples: "*My Father and I are one.*" Let us briefly allow these words of the Lord to have an effect on our inner being: "*My Father and I are one.*"

From these words of Jesus of Nazareth resonates an unspeakable love, an unspeakable trust in God, His and our Father. And this great love was also the devotion for us human beings, so that redemption could be accomplished. *"My Father and I are one"*— isn't it wonderful to be able to say that from the heart? We will surely soon have an excuse, "Well, I am a sinner, and as long as I have my sins, I am not one with my Father."

Let us turn it around and say it positively: "Deep in our soul is the eternally pure, our true *I Am*, what we are in God: pure beings. This pure being in me is one with my Father."

And now let's feel even more deeply into our inner being; let's leave aside the human being; let's leave aside the sins; instead we say it positively, because the innermost being in us is pure: "My Father and I are one." If we would more often foster and cultivate these sentiments that we basically are pure beings in the innermost part of our soul, beings who are one with the great love, who are one with God, our Father, then we would far more quickly repent of our recognized sins with the great help and love of the Redeemer. We would clear them up and no longer do them, and in this way keep the commandments, as Jesus commanded us. He said, *"Keep My commandments!"*

We people have the habit of always looking at the negative and always belittling ourselves with words or thoughts like, "Oh, well, we are all sinners!" When we say this over and over again, we are affirming that we are sinners, and in doing so, we are saying to ourselves, "Yes, we can only sin."—No, we must realize in our innermost being that we are all sons and daughters of God's great love, and in our innermost being we are united with God. And this unity with God should permeate our lives, so that we make use of the days and say to ourselves, "So, here again a sin, a burden breaks out, my thoughts are not thoughts of resurrection; Lord, I regret these thoughts and clear them up with You."

If we have negative thoughts toward our fellow people or if we have acted wrongly, then we say, "Christ, help me—my way of acting, my thoughts shall now be resurrected in You." We clear this up with our neighbor and thus make friends with our brother, with our sister—that is, we live like brothers and sisters.

In this way, we draw closer to this consciousness, this high consciousness, that Jesus, the Christ expressed again and again: *"My Father and I are one."* That is the resurrection; that is then the Good News. Jesus lives. Christ in me and I with Him.

Recommended Reading

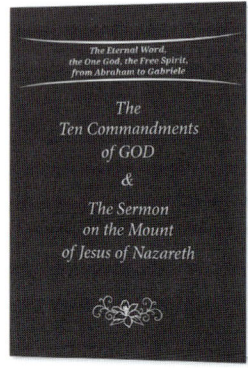

The Ten Commandments of GOD

&

The Sermon on the Mount of Jesus of Nazareth

Everything that we need to live in peace with one another and in unity with nature and the animals was already given to us thousands of years ago: They are the universal values that are contained for all people in the Ten Commandments of God and in the Sermon on the Mount of Jesus of Nazareth.

The Sermon on the Mount, however, is dismissed as utopian, and the Ten Commandments are changed or simply ignored as desired. Yet these fundamental principles have nothing to do with religions or churches. Rather, they are much more excerpts from the eternal law of the love for God and neighbor and apply to all people regardless of faith, culture or nationality. And one thing is very clear: They are not utopian, but quite livable, and lead to an inner peace and contentment and help us grow closer to God, the Free Spirit in us, step by step.

224 pp., SB, Order No. S182TBEN, ISBN: 978-3-96446-264-0
Also available as an E-book

This Is My Word
A and Ω

The Gospel of Jesus

The Christ-Revelation,
which True Christians the World Over
Have Come to Know

Jesus of Nazareth founded no religion. He installed no priests and taught no dogmas, rites or cults. 2000 years ago, He brought the truth from the Kingdom of God: the teachings of the love for God and neighbor toward people, nature and animals, the teaching of freedom, of peace and unity. He spoke about the God of love, of the Free Spirit—God in us.

In the mighty work of revelation, "This Is My Word – Alpha and Omega," Christ speaks from the Kingdom of God about the past, the present and the future through Gabriele, the prophetess and emissary of God.

In His work, which is a historic work, He directs Himself to all people, to explain what He as Jesus of Nazareth taught, how His life on Earth took its course, and He shows the correlations in the great work of redemption that has its origin in the Kingdom of God.

Hardbound: 1120 pp., Order No. S 007en, ISBN 978-3-96446-313-5
*Included is an audio CD with the eternal word from the Kingdom of God:
"The Call of the Christ of God" and "The Appearance."*
Softbound: 1120 pp., Order No. S007TBEN, ISBN 978-3-96446-310-4
Also available as an E-book

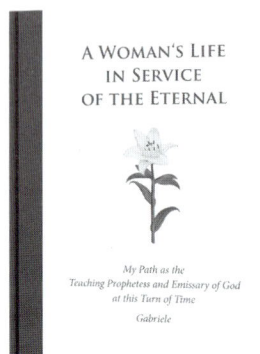

A Woman's Life in Service of the Eternal

My Path as
the Teaching Prophetess
and Emissary of God
at this Turn of Time

Gabriele

For over 45 years, Gabriele has served God, the Eternal, as His teaching prophetess and emissary. In her autobiographical descriptions, she gives insight into her development as a person and her call to be the prophetess of God and what it means to bring His Word, His Love and Wisdom to the Earth at this time. In a lively way, Gabriele describes her path through life from early childhood on. She describes the beginnings of the prophetic word, the direct schoolings from the Spirit of God and developing the worldwide work of the Christ of God. She also reports about the adversities and attacks that she withstood as a woman in service of the Eternal.

204 pp., HB, Order No. S 551en, ISBN 978-3-89201-814-8

**We will be glad to send you
our current catalog of books, CDs and DVDs,
as well as free excerpts on many different topics**

Gabriele Publishing House – The Word
P.O. Box 2221, Deering, NH 03244, USA
North America: Toll-Free No. 1-844-576-0937
International Orders: +49-9391-504-843
www.Gabriele-Publishing-House.com